Authe

GW00702807

Yo...

Developing the Authentic self

To DEAR LIZ,

THANK YOU FOR ALL THE
WONDERFUL CHATS AND
LAUGHTER!
WITH LOVE
Shuri x

Shuri Morgan-Radford
The Consciousness Architect

Moyhill Publishing

First Published in 2012 by *Moyhill* Publishing
Simple but Authentic drawings by Shuri Morgan-Radford

A CIP catalogue record for this book is available from the British Library.

ISBN 978-1-905597-34-5

Designed & typeset by *Moyhill* Publishing.

Printed in UK.

The papers used in this book were produced in an environmental friendly way from sustainable forests.

Moyhill Publishing,
Suite 471, 6 Slington House, Rankine Rd., Basingstoke, RG24 8PH, UK

A WORD OR TWO...!

A massive, tremendous, huge, enormous, gigantic, immense, colossal, very big, substantial, considerable, great, vast, mammoth and giant

'THANK YOU'

to the following people from the bottom of my heart for their contribution to this tome (even though some of you may not even know that you lent a hand!)

Daryl Morgan-Radford (my hubby); for adding your suggestions for positive changes. For your patience, tolerance, support, understanding and downright loveliness!

Suzie Sharpe (my friend for a lot of years); for your strength, inspiration, superb advice and being an all-round splendid person.

Allison Marlowe (my mentor & friend); for your advice, support and belief in me and for being a fine example to all business women.

David Cronin (my editor); for his patience, knowledge and being a thoroughly likeable chap!

Treacle (my cat); for your simple, Authentic and highly fluffy self!

Sam, Mrs White, The power lines, The new age group, The mask, Mum, The 50's actress, Himself, A friend, Cliff Young, Duncan, Gweny, Coma man, The relative, A guy, The young friend, The Ukrainian beach; for providing food for thought for my 'Story Time' segments.

Contents

INTRODUCTION

When I set out to write this book one of the most important things that I knew was that each of us has to be our true, original and Authentic self in order to really experience life to the full. With that in mind I started this introduction and before I had even written one page I realised that I had already begun to follow other people's rules about how to write a book! I wasn't being my Authentic self at all! It's tough sometimes to remain true to yourself in the face of other people's opinions particularly if those people are close to you. It can also be difficult to remain Authentic when the world seems to be against you. However, I wasn't going to be beaten! As a consequence you will find that I have broken some of the cardinal 'rules' when writing this book! It's fun to be Authentic isn't it!

This book is me being true to myself. In these pages I talk in a very no-nonsense, frank and honest way about the things that are important to me and I have a sneaking suspicion that you might well find that they are important to you also! So don't expect stacks of jargon or flouncy, flowery words! This book is a way of making change happen and as such it will appeal to the side of you that says 'I'm a busy, man/woman who has enough to do already so I need something that is easy to read, won't take ages and will really help me in my life!'

There is a growing awareness that our world needs to change. Once, it was just those who considered themselves 'spiritual' or 'religious' who knew that change must happen but increasingly it's 'everyman' who knows that Humanity has somehow got it 'wrong.' Whether it's dissatisfaction with those who make the rules or an undercurrent of discontentment in their own lives, most people have a slow, low rumbling that something needs to change.

In my line of work, as The Consciousness Architect, I have many people expressing the fact that the world feels like a coiled spring or an elastic band about to snap. Individuals are beginning to see that this is more than just stress or fear; they feel it stems from something much, much bigger and I agree with their view. I believe that what we are all experiencing is a recognition that the very foundations of our thinking processes are at fault. The structures in place in our society which are born out of those ways of thinking are beginning to break down. Change is needed and it is needed NOW.

So, do you know how we can begin to really make a change? The majority of people have very little idea. In fact, they often say, 'I don't think I could do anything on my own.' Oh how wrong they are! One person can make a MASSIVE difference to the world; providing that they are coming from their own place of Authenticity. Being your own person; your own unique, individual self is becoming a vital part of world change.

So why start with Authenticity?

Well, the simple answer is that when you come from a place of Authenticity, you are coming from a much deeper level; you are working from the level of the Higher Mind and the great irony of Authenticity is that the more you concentrate on your own needs the more you will be servicing humanity. By being true to yourself and doing what has real meaning for you, you are putting yourself in a much more productive and resourceful space and life becomes easier and more joyful. But much more than that is that when your own decisions for your life are coming from that deeper place, the desire to manipulate or change others becomes obsolete. Who wouldn't want that?

We were born with a brain to think and a mind to create and potential motivation to make all manner of amazing things happen but those abilities are being eroded by society's need to control, to regulate, to structure and to manage. A lot of people are now finding it very hard to live in what is their unique and Authentic self because of the limiting crush of the way things 'should' be. You may even ask 'aren't I always being true to myself?' Well, the answer to that is 'No you're probably not.' Society is now so indoctrinated with rules and regulations, should do's and ought to's, influences and affectations that you probably aren't even aware of the ways in which you aren't being your true self.

Within these pages I am giving you the wealth of my experience – that's 30-odd years (and sometimes they really have been odd!) of mentoring, teaching, coaching, training and facilitating a vast plethora of subjects (please see my website for more information on these) all of which have, in some way, been connected to the way we work as Human Beings. My Authentic self is – and always has been – fascinated by what makes us tick, by how we can develop our highest self and by how to bring out the very best in people. My experience had taught me that being true to yourself should be a FUNDAMENTAL way of living. It should be taught in schools and encouraged. However, instead, we are living in a world that constantly categorises and divides. Driven by economics rather than human needs, we are herded about like so many lost sheep and we are beginning to lose our identities. All of this is gravely to our detriment. So, my passion is to bring individuality back to people; to remind them that they do have a choice, that we can all be who we want to be regardless of what is going on 'out there'. Does that seem unreal to you? Well I'm here to tell you that it is perfectly possible and I will show you how in the pages of this book. More and more people are realising the need for change and I'm sure that you are well aware that when enough people want something to happen and that desire reaches a critical mass, then remarkable things begin to happen.

Maybe you don't want to make a massive difference to the world. Maybe you would just like to be able to enjoy life a bit more or actually pay the bills without worrying. *Whatever* you want to change, this book is written for YOU. If you feel any sense of discontent, whether it is in your life or in the world then I am talking to you. If you even have an inkling that there could be a different way to do things – turn your attention this way! If you have a burning sense of frustration that you have something important to do with your life, I want to have a word in your shell-like (that's ear to you)! If you have a great job/partner/kids/home etc but still ache for something else, read this book! If you are ready to make changes to yourself, to be a better person, I wrote this book for you!

This is not a straightforward self-help book as such. Neither is it a philosophical, spiritual or mystical book. It is none of those, yet all of those. I don't mean to confuse you but I do mean to intrigue you! If you are intrigued then you are curious and the one thing that I ask of you, as you read this book, is that you remain curious, open-minded and ready to challenge yourself on the ideas about life and humanity that you already have.

Now – this book may seem to you to jump around a lot. It is done that way for a reason. Please do NOT skip around in the book. Read it from cover to cover and take your time over it. Also you will find quite a bit of repetition in some places. Again, this is done for a purpose. Both methods allow your mind to hear and understand what you are reading and discovering. How many times do we apparently hear something but don't hear it at all?! Do you recognise the phrase 'How many times do I have to tell you…?'! It isn't just children that need to hear something several times. We adults do too!

It is also vitally important that answer the questions as you go. Make sure that you have a notebook to write down your answers. I would also suggest that you record any thoughts that occur to you along the way. These may well prove invaluable.

And finally, in this book I don't always give you the answers (yes – frustrating isn't it!). Sometimes you will have to discover them for yourself. In a world where everyone has someone to think for them whether it be politicians, health officials, the media (not to mention our own friends and family!) I want you to really make decisions for yourself. So I have no intention of mollycoddling you! To be your Authentic self, you need to think for yourself. Please be aware that I don't mean to be patronising. As you go through the book you may be surprised at how little thinking you actually do for yourself; and influence comes from so many sources. But, if you don't THINK for yourself, you can't DO for yourself and consequently BE your unique and Authentic self. Do you see my point?

So – welcome to my words and my world. It is my pleasure to bring you my thoughts and I sincerely hope that you enjoy them. The very fact that you are about to turn the page makes *me* intrigued about who *you* are. Maybe one day we will meet…

Thank you for your presence of mind.

See you soon…

Shuri Morgan-Radford

AN AUTOBIOGRAPHY IN 5 SHORT CHAPTERS

I

I walk down the street. There is a deep hole in the sidewalk.
I fall in. I am lost… I am helpless. It isn't my fault.
It takes forever to find a way out.

II

I walk down the same street. There is a deep hole in the sidewalk.
I pretend I don't see it. I fall in again. I can't believe
I am in the same place. But it isn't my fault.
It still takes a long time to get out.

III

I walk down the street. There is a deep hole in the sidewalk.
I see it is there. I still fall in. It's a habit but my eyes are open.
I know where I am. It is my fault.
I get out immediately.

IV

I walk down the same street again.
There is a deep hole in the sidewalk.
I walk around it.

V

I walk down another street.
The End.

by Portia Nelson

Yesterday

(a far less well known poem by Shuri Morgan-Radford!)

Yesterday I ate some Marmite.
Today I ate some Marmite and
didn't really enjoy it.
Tomorrow I'll have Jam.

That's a simple kind of process. We all recognise it and we've all done it at some point in our lives. I don't mean giving up Marmite for an alternative spread (although maybe you have done that)! I mean that we've had a realization that something isn't right for us and instantly made a decision to change. Sometimes, as with the Portia Nelson poem, it takes a few tries to make the change but we all recognise that process – yes? However, sometimes it isn't that we don't recognise the need for change, we really, really do but we feel that we CAN'T change for one reason or another. We feel stuck, disempowered, having no choice, unable to move an inch. The stuck feeling is quite often more to do with habits and behaviours that have gotten deeply embedded, sometimes since childhood.

Being your true self, your unique self, living in your own skin, being comfortable in your own body, being in your right mind, being your Authentic self can be as simple as changing from Marmite to jam; but often it's more like stopping falling down a deep hole in the sidewalk!

However, don't let that stop you. It's time for change…

Section 1: BEING MIGHTY REAL!

Once at a party I asked someone 'So, what do you do?' He reached into his pocket, handed me a 'business' card which had his name on it and underneath was written 'Human Being' and his telephone number! I loved it! He didn't define himself by his job, he just 'was'! It meant that I had to take him on face value and the only judgement I could make (if I found it necessary to judge that is!) was on the person I saw before me. It really was a big lesson for me and it got me thinking about who I truly was? I 'did' Mentoring; I 'did' Life Coaching etc, etc but who was I when it just came to 'being'? It's a difficult one to answer isn't it? We are so used to talking about what we 'do' rather than what we are, but of course what we do, if we get it right, will reflect who we are. We will be doing the things that have meaning for us and, therefore, being who we are and sometimes it is as simple as that; then other times it isn't…

How often in your life have you said something like 'I'm doing **X** for the moment but it isn't really me?' or 'Well I just have to put up with **Y** even though it's not what I would choose' or 'I'm doing **Z** but my heart's really not in it'? These are the times that you really aren't being 'you' and that's ok in the short term – we all do things that aren't really 'us' to get us to where we want to be – but if you are doing it long-term then you will begin to suffer in spiritual, emotional, mental and eventually physical ways. In other words, if the things we 'do' aren't congruent with the person we 'are' then we will pay the price.

The irony about the 'being self' is that it will probably have shown itself in your childhood. Then as we grow we are driven by outside influences to curtail our dreams and 'get real'! If it carries on being stifled it will show itself through daydreams and fantasy in the adult life. Then we tend to see all of those things as unimportant and 'just' stupid childishness. But our day-dreaming contains elements of the things that we hold dear to us. It shows us what we feel we have to offer and what we feel our life is 'about' – and for each of us it is different.

So don't ignore the moments when your mind is just floating; it is working out possibilities. It is giving you some information about what your Authentic self would 'love' to do and be. You may be daydreaming of being Prime Minister which doesn't necessarily mean that you want to put the current incumbent out of a job! However, looking at what is involved in that role will show you what excites you and 'floats your boat'. It might need some exploring and it might take a while to work out how this will manifest in your life but when you do make it work your deeper self will say 'this is exactly how I wanted my life to 'BE'!'

Your Turn: Great Expectations!

The following questions are related to your thoughts and feelings about the book that you are about to experience. Please be brutally honest in your answers as honesty will help you to get the most out of the book. NO ONE need see anything that you write in your notebook.

   a) What made you want to read this book?
   b) What are you expecting from it?
   c) What would you like to see happen from it?
   d) What positive things would you like to get from reading it?

Story-time!

I charge about like a headless chicken with reckless abandon for reasons that no one else can understand.

I wash when it pleases me, which is often.

I'm obsessed with biscuits.

I always stay away from people I don't like or that upset me.

I love to sleep for hours in the warm sunshine.

I love to explore but sometimes bite off more than I can chew.

I wear my fur coat with pride.

I am truly Authentic.

I am Treacle the Cat.

Here's some news; the power to make the changes are within YOUR hands alone. I have written the book but it's up to you to put the words into action. Yes, I know that you knew that already but how many times in the past have you said 'I'm going to do X' then never done it? Well 'TODAY IS THE FIRST DAY OF THE REST OF YOUR LIFE' as the famous 60's saying goes and I invite you to make those changes starting from NOW!

Section 2: THE POWER OF AUTHENTICITY

I don't want to do this!

How often do you say to yourself *I really don't want to be here* or *I don't want to be doing this*? How often do you find yourself saying 'yes' to someone when actually you mean 'no'? How many times do you find yourself crossing your own bottom line? Do you even have a bottom line? If you recognise these things going on in your life, it may well be because you are not being your Authentic self. Being Authentic means being unique. It means living your life your own way and not following another person's way of doing things. It means being confident and self-assured enough to do what makes you happy and fulfilled so that you get the maximum out of life's experiences.

Square peg in a round hole!

If you aren't living in your own skin and in a way that is natural to you, you will constantly feel like a stretched elastic band. You may feel that you are a 'square peg in a round hole' or 'stuck in the mud.' You may feel as though you don't 'fit' anywhere. You may find yourself spending a lot of hours in the day doing things which don't feel natural to you, or make you sad or unhappy or which just plain annoy you. Whatever you feel, it won't be pleasant. You will struggle on but will never really feel 'right.' You may even get ill, drink too much, find it difficult to relax and generally find life tough.

I feel great!

So why is it important to be your Authentic self? Well, living in your own skin means that you are doing what is right for you. You are being driven by your own values and desires and therefore your life will have more meaning and be much more fulfilling. Communication becomes easier as you stop feeling as though you are pretending to be someone else. You make your own decisions on what you know to be right or wrong for you. You will be happy to listen to someone's advice but ultimately will make your own informed decisions.

You will feel more confident and have more self-esteem. You will know your worth and you will feel altogether more secure. Although it is about pleasing yourself, it isn't about being selfish. Think of the analogy of the plane crash. We are told that in the event of the air masks coming down, we must put on our own before our children's. Authenticity is like that. When we know that we are secure then we are in a good position to help others.

Feel the fear and…!

Some people say to me 'but I'm too scared to go out there and do what I really want to do.' My answer is always that there are times when there is fear attached to doing something but your Authentic self will say 'I'm scared but I really want to do this.' The more that you can 'Feel the fear and do it anyway' as the author Susan Jeffers says, the more fulfilled and strong your Authentic self will become. Practice makes perfect in this case! And sometimes you may find that what you thought you wanted to do or be isn't actually what you wanted at all! But that's ok. – at least you are one step closer to knowing your real self by knowing one more thing that isn't Authentic to you! This is when the really good changes begin to take place.

Weird man!

Being unique and Authentic for some people means not running with the herd; it means being different than the norm – but that's a good thing. Other people may find it strange that you are behaving differently at first (particularly those close to you) but soon they will begin to respect that you are making your own choices. Some people may even think that your ideas and ways are odd, but you will unconsciously be giving other people the message that we don't all have to be clones. By your actions you will be giving others the permission to live Authentically. Also your contentment will be their evidence that you are making good choices in your life.

Dynamic!

It's also important to mention that being your Authentic self is a dynamic thing! It is fluid and changeable and you may find that what was unique and individual to you last year, isn't the same today. You must make allowance for growth and natural change within your Authenticity.

It's a bit like that item of clothing that you find at the back of the wardrobe which was so special at one time but which now you wouldn't be seen dead in! So just love finding out who you are and what you can do today and don't worry if that changes tomorrow!

The power of it all!

Being your Authentic self is a **powerful** thing. By your authenticity you are connecting to your Higher Self and life inevitably becomes much more rewarding. When you understand and start acting in an Authentic way you are better able to let go of anger, jealously, envy, fear, insecurity and all of those other unproductive emotions because you are doing what you want to do with your life. (Please note: there is a difference between anger and righteous anger – more on this later.) Living in and appreciating the moment becomes more important than dwelling in the past or the future. Real contentment, love, compassion and understanding enter your life.

If each of us committed to living Authentically what would happen to the world then…? Happier people with more energy and zest for life; less stress, less anger, more tolerance…the list goes on!

That's a powerful thing, isn't it…!

So – could you choose to find your Authentic self today – right now? Could you give your true opinion, dress in a particular way, take up a hobby, do something that you've been dying to do for years? Start to create your own future. Whatever it is, do it in the knowledge that each time you make a personal choice and act on it, it will feel more and more natural because it is already part of you. Go forth in Authenticity!

Your Turn: 'Reality'

Answer these questions and notice what your answers make you feel and think:-

Who do you know that seems truly Authentic?
Who have you met that is truly living in their own skin?
Who appears to you to be really 'real'?
Who in your circle of acquaintances is just going for what they know to be true?
Who strikes you as being 'a round peg in a round hole' n your life?
Who, in your opinion, exudes confidence by being their true self?
How do you know that any of these people are being real?
How do you feel about them?
What do you think about them?
What do you admire about them?
How would you like to be like them?
When would you like to start?

Section 3: HONESTY IS THE BEST POLICY

'So what about this book of questions then Shuri?' I hear you saying! Well, it's already started! But before we continue, I'd like you to make some promises to yourself.

a) As you are going through this book of questions, I would like you to be truly honest with yourself. Not the kind of honest that says 'I'll consider that later' or 'I can't admit that' or 'That's too frightening' but the honesty that says 'If I tell the truth to myself, no matter how challenging, I will be happier, healthier and less stressed'. Seeking the Authentic self does mean that there will be occasions when the best decision is the hardest one; but do you want to see what life is like when you are relaxed and enjoying what you do and how you spend your time?

b) Learn the information and USE IT rather than just making this a cerebral exercise. If you simply read the words but never put it all into practice it will remain in your head rather than in your body and therefore your lifestyle.

c) It is also really important to have a book or a folder that you can write thoughts in and complete exercises as you go through the book. (Yes, I know I've already said it, but I wonder how many of you have actually done it!) This tells your subconscious that you really do want to learn and make changes. Immediately taking things out of your head and putting them into the world is way more powerful than you can imagine! No one need see what you write in your note book so you can be brutally honest if necessary.

d) There will come a time (and I hope it's sooner rather than later) that you will begin to make changes that will effect, not just your life, but those around you. These changes will bring different responses from different people in your life, but never fear! This book will also show you how to deal with the fallout both negative and positive and believe me, there will be plenty of positive fallout!

So – let's truly begin the journey to Authenticity…

Section 4: RIVER OF THE MIND

(How we turn dreams into reality)

Picture this...

Let me start by taking you through a process that happens to us all every day in one form or another. You will recognise it...

(*Ann feels hunger pangs*) I'm hungry. What shall I have for lunch?

(*She imagines different kinds of foods*) What have I got?'

(*She imagines contents of cupboards and fridge*) A cheese sandwich? Don't fancy that.

(*She imagines alternative food. Licks lips*) Mmmm... Spanish omelette.

(*She goes to kitchen. Takes out the food necessary to make omelette. Makes omelette*)

(*She eats omelette*) Mmmm...lovely!

If we split this scenario up into its component parts we might have this –

1: NEED/DESIRE

(*Ann feels hunger pangs*) I'm hungry. What shall I have for lunch?

2: IMAGINATION

(*She imagines different kinds of foods*) What have I got?'

(*She imagines contents of cupboards and fridge*) A cheese sandwich? Don't fancy that.

(*She imagines alternative food. Licks lips*) Mmmm...Spanish omelette.

3: ACTION

(*She goes to kitchen. Takes out the food necessary to make omelette. Makes omelette*)

(*She eats omelette*) Mmmm...lovely!

Obviously this is simplifying the process but basically the **Action (3)** stems from a **Need or Desire (1)** and it is the **Imagination (2)** that solves the problem of how to do it. Everything we do in life could be said to go through this 3-Step Plan. Some things happen so fast (as in the scenario above) that we are unaware of the process. Other things, such as redecorating a house, can happen so slowly that we are all too aware of the process! However, providing that we go from (1) to (2) to (3) we are relatively happy because we are getting the things that we want or need; in other words, we are turning our dreams into reality. It's when things don't go that smoothly that the problems start.

Sometimes **Needs and Desires** remain just that because the desire wanes to the extent that it has become weak and is no longer a priority. The goal may have seemed important at one particular time but its significance has died. If this is the case then we are caused no anguish by that loss of movement forwards. However, if the **Desire** (1) is alive and strong, it will then need to move on to the **Imagination** (2) stage. This stage involves the planning, decision making and envisioning the achievement of the goal. Providing that the **Need** is great and the **Imagination** is there, you will be able to think of ways of making it happen, thereby solving any challenges that arise and therefore move (in time) to achievement of the goal via the **Action** (3) stage.

It is the Imagination stage that is make or break in the process. The feelings and thoughts that you have at this point ensures smooth running into the Action stage or makes for a dead stop. If there is excessive fear or personal beliefs that are limiting your progress, you CANNOT move on to the Action stage. Something has to change or be clearly understood until the blockage can be removed. To understand this more, we need to look at the **Imagination** (2) in greater detail.

Stuck in the middle...

Now study the figure below: it's one of the most important things to know if you are in search of your Authentic self. There are many ways to view how the mind works. This is just one, very simplified way but it can be a useful tool in order to see how the mind operates and particularly how we can block ourselves from turning our dreams into reality.

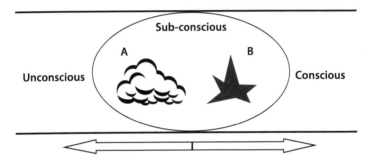

The Unconscious =

The "Higher" mind, the "soul" or the part of us that is connected to the Universe/God/energy force (call it what you wish). This part does not judge and is linked to our intuition. It is the awe we feel on seeing a sunrise. It houses our deeper sense of belonging to something greater than just ourselves. It is also the part of us that feels the connection to the whole of humanity.

The Subconscious =

This is the part that takes in everything that we do, say, hear and see. It works in symbols and shows through our dreams. Underlying feelings and thoughts are here in what I like to call Jagged Sharps (Negative information) & Fluffy Softs (Positive information)! It is where the blueprint for our existence is fundamentally made. It could be said to house our imagination. The Subconscious believes everything it 'sees' and does not edit and herein lies its challenge to us.

The Conscious Mind =

The part with which we "talk" to ourselves. It is our everyday thinking that we could call our "chatterbox" in our head. It's what we "hear" when we are quiet.

A = A Fluffy Soft (more in next paragraph!)

B = A Jagged Sharp (ditto!)

The mind should flow freely (hence the arrows) from the unconscious through the subconscious to the conscious and vice versa. However, as we go through life, thoughts (based on the things that we have done, said, heard, seen and felt) enter our subconscious from the conscious mind. The subconscious does not edit; it 'believes' everything. It also cannot 'understand' a negative command. Let me give you an example. Don't think of a bright pink elephant. Did you imagine a bright pink elephant? Well let me tell you that you will have imagined a bright pink elephant whether you realised it or not! (Our minds don't always work in pictures; some people will have words, or even a feeling or sound of that elephant!) The mind won't have registered the 'Don't…' part of that command and will go straight to the 'think' part itself! That is why if you want someone to remember something, you should never start your command with 'Don't forget…' because the command you are giving will be received as 'Forget…'!

Add to this the power of the subconscious even on our physical bodies…

Your Turn: Juicy, Juicy Lemon!

Read through this slowly, making the image stronger and stronger and highly detailed as you go.

> Imagine a fat, juicy lemon.
> Place it in your hand.
> Study its shape.
> Really consider how heavy it is in your hand.
> Look at its dimpled yellow skin.
> Feel it with your fingers.
> Is the lemon warm or cold on your skin?
> Place that fat, juicy lemon on a cutting board.
> Take a knife and cut that lemon in half.
> Look at the yellow flesh.
> See the scattering of white pips.
> See the juice running from where it's been cut.
> Lift that lemon and really breathe in its sharp scent.
> Now, open your mouth and take a great big bite out of that fat, juicy, sharp, citrusy lemon.

What happened? Did you begin to salivate? (It's very likely that you did. If you didn't; try the exercise again but add more of your own details.) That is the power that the subconscious has on the body. If your subconscious believes that you are eating the lemon your body will respond accordingly. Food for thought isn't it…?

You can see from the exercise above that **the power of the subconscious is total**. It can affect everything that happens in your life from physical responses to emotional reactions to thought processes. Compliments and criticisms in particular can colour our thought processes. For example – if as a child someone said 'you are pretty' then there is a potential that it will have created, what I like to call (in a purely fun way you understand!) a 'Fluffy Soft' (A) in the subconscious which will have a subsequent positive effect. You may then spend the remainder of your life feeling confident about the way you look.

If, on the other hand, as a child A. N. Other said 'you are a lazy good-for-nothing' then a 'Jagged Sharp' (B) will have potentially been created which has a negative effect and can prevent you from ever seeing yourself as anything but lazy. Relaxing may then prove a problem for you because you see it as laziness.

So, imagine that a Fluffy Soft is like a beautiful fluffy cloud of cotton wool which thoughts can move through and bounce over and which strengthen the thought. Imagine a clear illuminated pathway along which the thoughts can freely move. Now imagine that the Jagged Sharp is like a lethal piece of black glass that doesn't let anything through. In contrast, this would be a maze which is in total darkness through which the thoughts blindly stagger. Whilst the Fluffy Softs encourage a creative train of thought, the Jagged Sharps stop them in their tracks.

Obviously, this is a grossly simplified version of events because Jagged Sharps and Fluffy Softs get overlaid, crossed, reinforced and wiped out on a never-ending and continuous basis. The configuration changes throughout our lives as we have more and more experiences. The Jagged Sharps or Fluffy Softs get stronger or weaker depending on those experiences and are dependant not just on other people's opinions but our growing opinions of ourselves. However, the principle remains – if you have plenty of Fluffy Softs regarding an issue, you will find it easy to take the third step of Action but if you have too many Jagged Sharps concerning an issue (limiting beliefs) then you will find it difficult to put thoughts into action. Your limiting beliefs are preventing you from taking your Needs/Desires to the end of the cycle into Action.

I can't get no satisfaction...

People create all manner of 'reasons' for not doing things – no money, no time, don't have the necessary skills, don't have the qualifications and sometimes these things are true, but more often than not it is actually fear (a Jagged Sharp, a limiting belief) that is holding them back.

In the scene at the beginning of this section, you have the **Need** or **Desire**, followed by the **Imagination**, finished off with the **Action**. If the imagination is at odds with the desire ('I want to make a Spanish omelette for lunch but I can't cook') then the action will not follow. Sometimes, it is down to lack of skills but what if our lady Ann was always told that she was simply incapable of cooking? The result would be the same – the desire, the imagination but no subsequent action. She may even find it hard to contemplate (Imagine) carrying out the action and would probably remain 'unable' to cook for the rest of her life. Add to this is the fact that many of us have limiting beliefs that we don't even know are there! We want to do something but can't work out *why* we don't just do it!

Unless something changes to remove the belief that limits you from trying, you will remain 'stuck'.

I have a dream…

If you have a dream that doesn't seem to be making its way into reality, you will need to understand what those Jagged Sharps are that are blocking your subconscious; but be kind to yourself. Anger, strain and self judgement does not work well in this situation. Gentle persuasion does. By gently looking at your subconscious you will discover – and indeed, uncover – a whole lot of important information as to why you cannot move forwards.

Ask yourself what are the real issues underlying your blockage and when the answer comes (and it will if you remain true to yourself and listen with patience) then you can begin to remove the obstacles. Almost invariably there will be some kind of fear attached to achieving the dream. Discover what it is then (without the self-flagellation!) gently move in the direction of the dream in small steps. Keep reminding yourself that there is nothing actually stopping you but you. The Universe wants to provide you with your dreams not hinder you and there are vast possibilities out there to help you on your way.

Your life is only as great as your **Desire** and **Imagination**. It is up to you to take the **Action**. Be bold; be gentle on yourself but take that action and you will be surprised at just how easy it was after all.

So what bearing does all of this have on the Authentic self? Well – it is VITAL. Throughout this book I will be referring to your Jagged Sharps and Fluffy Softs because it is the way you allow those to operate that will determine whether you will truly be the Authentic person that you were born to be. Later on I shall be showing you ways to combat the Jagged Sharps and turn them into Fluffy Softs but right now I want you to notice the part of your mind that says that you can't do things. Become aware of how many times you say something or think something that could stop you from achieving the round peg, round hole you. You don't have to berate yourself, but it is important to quietly notice.

When I say 'quietly' I truly mean quietly and calmly. Nothing can be achieved by going like a 'bull at a gate'! The message that you will give your subconscious if you do is that you are desperate and what does that create? Correct! A Jagged Sharp.

Your Turn: How Authentic Are You?

Answer the following questions as honestly as you can. Remember that the more honest you are, the better the changes that you can make to your life. Don't just imagine the answers, write them down. Writing them down represents 'taking immediate action' and will be a message to your subconscious that you mean business. Also, if you date each **Your Turn**, it will act as a reference to you as you begin to change things in your life and become more Authentic.

1. Do you spend the majority of your day doing what you choose to do?

2. What things do you feel obligated to do? Who or what tells you that you must?

3. How often do you follow other people's advice against your own better judgment?

4. Is your work/play/rest in balance and at a level that makes you feel content?

5. What do you love doing? How often do you do it?

6. Do you have peace of mind a good deal of the time? What takes away your peace of mind?

7. Do you feel content with who you are?

8. Can you say 'no' when you know you need to? What stops you?

9. Do you frequently feel the need to judge other people?

10. How much do other people's opinions affect you?

11. How often do you feel angry?

12. Do you take responsibility for the things that you do?

13. Are you true to yourself?

14. Is moaning a large part of your conversation?

15. Do you automatically take media stories to heart and let it affect you?

16. How often do you find yourself thinking 'this really isn't me' but doing/saying/feeling it anyway?

17. What 'masks' (i.e. confidante, cash machine, grin and bear it, martyr) do you wear that you feel don't belong to you?

18. Do you have the feelings that you want to have most of the time?

19. What 'floats your boat' big time and when do you allow yourself to do that?

20. Would your child self feel proud of your adult self?

21. Would you choose to walk a mile in your own shoes?

22. What action can you take to change just one small thing and when is NOW a good time to make that change?

And now let's look at the next vital thing on your path to Authenticity.

Section 5: THE 4 LEVELS OF BEING

Look closely at the figure below...

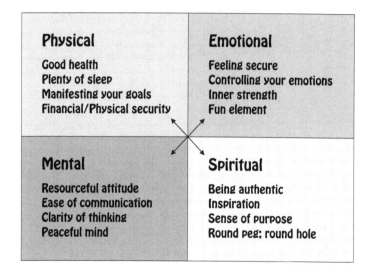

Our being is made up of 4 levels.

All of the levels stand alone but also work together. In other words, we can see all of the levels in action separately but each one is totally interactive with the others. Therefore, we could also view them in this way:

Four Levels of Being

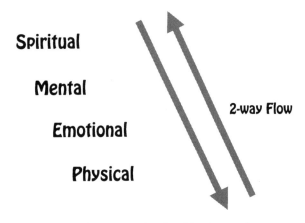

Every level has an effect on another level (and sometimes even more than one). Witness this when you are doing something that you hate doing. You feel 'low in spirit,' your mind is 'numb', you are emotionally 'angry as hell' and eventually your physical self will display signs of dis-ease. We are sophisticated people these days. We all know that this happens. We talk freely of stress causing illness and 'the weight of the world on our shoulders' causing neck pain. But how often do we do something about it?! It is important that there is an alignment with each of these levels.

Today <u>you</u> are going to take action…

Your Turn: What Are My Needs?

Take a look again at the 4 levels and write down what you feel you need for each level. Remember that this is not an exercise in what everyone else thinks you need (including well-meaning health officials!) it's what you have discovered for yourself. Some questions you may not be able to answer. Some things may need some personal research and by that I mean taking more notice of yourself. Don't worry if you don't have all of the answers to the questions right away; the very fact that you have considered it will start activating your mind to find the answer.

On the Physical level I need...

Look at – the diet that keeps you healthy, how much exercise you need and what type, how much sleep you feel you need, how much money you need to feel secure.

On the Emotional level I need...

Look at – what makes you emotionally secure, what helps you to stay calm, what makes you feel strong, how do you need to have fun and relax.

On the Mental level I need...

Look at – what helps you to have a resourceful attitude, what helps you to communicate easily, what you need to keep your thoughts clear and fresh, what makes your mind still and quiet.

On the Spiritual level I need...

Look at – what makes you feel comfortable in your own skin, what gives you a sense of connection to other people, what inspires you and makes you want to get up in the morning.

Now – during this exercise you may have discovered more of what you don't want than what you do want! Great! Relish this moment! You are truly beginning to recognise who you are and it may be that you have too many of the things that you don't want in your life right now. Don't despair! Make a promise to yourself that you are going to recognise your needs on each level of your existence and make the changes that need to happen.

For example, if you need more sleep, start planning now. What do you need to do to get more sleep? Remember that you an individual with individual needs and only you can decide what is right for you. Despite everything that is written by people apparently 'in the know', I have always been a person who needs about 10 hours sleep per night. I work intensely (mentally and emotionally) and mostly in short bursts and that takes its toll on my physical self but it's the way I work at my optimum. As a result I often need more sleep, so that's what I take. No guilt, no moans (well – maybe I do feel some of these things some of the time – I'm only human!) but I know what is best for me. There is no such thing as the mass generalization that is constantly occurring in the media and by well-meaning do-gooders. You are unique and individual so you need to find your unique and individual needs.

Changing just one thing on any level has a knock on effect on all of the others up or down, whether that change is good or bad. Make a change for the good today – it need only be one small change – and witness the result.

Section 6: A STATEMENT OF FACT?

Are these statements right or wrong?

a) We don't make mistakes, we just have learning's.

b) If you do what you've always done, you'll get what you always got.

c) Take your life in your own hands and what happens? A terrible thing – no one to blame!

d) A human being is a single being. Unique and unrepeatable.

e) To change one's life: do it now; do it flamboyantly; no exceptions (no excuses).

f) You should always be aware that your head creates your world.

g) There is but one cause of human failure and that is Man's lack of faith in his true self.

Did you say 'yes' for all statements. Did you say 'no' for all, or a mixture of both?

Well actually there is no right or wrong answer. Whatever statement you believe will have an impact on your life. Your life is the external evidence of your internal declarations. Therefore your own statements, tenets, creeds should reflect the way that you choose to live your life. Yours may be religious or spiritual or just a phrase that you find yourself saying quite often! Whatever they are, make them resourceful; make them work for you.

I happen to believe in all of the statements given here. Do you have some statements of your own that you live by? If you haven't got any yet, these wouldn't be a bad place to start!

Section 7: WHAT'S THE PROBLEM?

'**H**ow is it so difficult to be my Authentic self?' you may ask, 'Aren't I always being myself?'

Well, the answer to that is probably 'No.' We are so indoctrinated with rules and regulations, should do's and ought to's, influences and affectations that you probably aren't even aware of the ways in which you aren't being yourself.

Here are just some of the people and things that can influence our choices:-

1. Parents
2. Siblings
3. Friends
4. Teachers
5. Priest
6. Advertisers
7. Mentors
8. Fashion
9. Partners
10. Television programmes
11. Well-wishers
12. Guilt
13. Obligation
14. Desire to be liked
15. Desire to fit in
16. (You fill this one in)
17. (You fill this one in)

We have become a society of people who are afraid to step outside of 'the norm' (who is this norm-guy anyway!) Even when we apparently do rebel we join other sheep-like groups of like-minded 'individuals'; witness the Hippie, the Punk, the Goth, the Emo!

There is, of course, a contradiction here. Human nature seeks a mate, a partner, a person or persons with whom we can share commonality. We want to belong and there is nothing wrong in wanting to belong; it's when that belonging happens at the cost to our self and others that something needs to be addressed. I'm not just talking here about the extremes of community such as gang or cult membership. The problem doesn't need to be that extreme. What I'm talking about the lengths to which many people will go just to fit in; the fear that being an individual brings to them which can make them alter their entire perspective on life. When this happens, poor decisions follow and poor action follows that. Before too long the fearful person will be living a life that doesn't actually belong to them remotely and all because of the desire to 'fit in'.

This is way more prevalent than many people seem to be aware of. Our world is moving more and more towards the need for perfection and is using the mechanism of conformity. Ironically, however, this isn't bringing greater contentment or fulfilment; in fact the effect is quite the opposite.

Your Turn: Ain't No Stopping Me Now!

1. Going through the list (page 32), write down some beliefs that you had from some of those influencers.

2. How many of those beliefs are outmoded and no longer serving you?

3. Make a note of a time (or even times) when you have done something against your true self because of one of these influences.

4. For each thing that you have written, ask yourself whether you can trust that influencer's opinion.

5. Ask yourself why did you fall into the trap of believing it to be true?

6. For each one, ask yourself what you now know and how you can prevent yourself from walking down the street with the hole in it again?

Your Turn: What Part Of 'No' Don't You Understand?

I'm pretty sure you will have heard of the saying above!

Now, I'm not suggesting that you adopt it verbatim (complete with stroppy vocals) but sometimes 'no' is the only answer to someone's question! It can be difficult to say but practice makes perfect. If someone is asking you to do something and you are really not sure that you want to/are able to/can do it, give yourself some breathing space to make a choice if you need to. Adopt a series of things that you might reply if necessary – 'I'll have to check if I'm available' or 'What does that entail?' or simply 'I can't make a decision right now but I'll let you know'. Don't, however, fall into the trap of simply putting off the inevitable and prolonging the agony. If you know that the answer is 'no' then say it; say it quickly and politely ('Sorry, I can't help you out.') and you do not have to give a reason although, at first, you may feel happier to give a reason.

The more you experience the 'no' word, the more confident you will feel about saying it. Ironically, people rarely value someone who constantly says 'yes'. In fact, 'yesers' are often taken for granted. So don't always be available, or be willing to put yourself out or compliant with other people's needs. Ask yourself this – 'Just because I can, does it mean I want/have to?'

(Long) Story-time!

I loathe social networking! (I mean the ones where people talk about what sandwich they had for lunch not the other ones!) I'll say it again! I loathe social networking! With a vengeance! I see it as unnecessary, a complete waste of time, self-indulgent, boring and pointless. I do not need friends to type to and people in my past are pretty much there for a reason! I'm aware that I am in the (not-so-small-as-you-might-think) minority! I'm also aware that it is a great comfort to many people!

BUT LISTEN UP FOLKS! I DO NOT **HAVE** TO LIKE SOCIAL NETWORKING! And if one more person tells me that I have to, I think I shall scream! (Calm down Shuri!)

The reason I don't like it apart from the reasons I've given above, is that I am not comfortable with a computer. Oh – I can type books and articles and create posters all day with no problem because it's creative but when it comes to learning how to use THOSE sites I am flummoxed! I once sat through a 2-hour seminar from a very lovely lady (Sam Russell 'The Facebook Queen') who obviously knew her stuff, copiously making notes but when I got home hey presto! 'Just click that button' translated itself into blip blop splink blat tock! Where was the wretched button anyway? Talking it though with my husband I discovered that for some reason I do not see what other people see on the web page. As a consequence it causes me palpitations, the shakes, exhaustion and a ringing in my head just from the effort of trying. In fact, it isn't even the trying to learn that causes that; it's the very act of using it. (Weirdly, I'm exactly the same with recipes, so I'm a lousy cook but no-one tries to badger me into that one!)

But here's the important bit – my Authentic self has absolutely NO DESIRE to learn to use SN. I do not find it 'easy' as everyone has told me; I do not 'love it when (I) get into it.' On the contrary – I've become more determined to manage without it. Oh if you put my name in you'll find me and I will probably say 'yes' to a friendship request but pretty much all you will see on there is a regular quote or two (because I've been shown how to get round that one) and very occasionally (when I can cope with it) some information. One day I may succumb to having someone operate the wretched thing for me and it will be someone whose Authentic self 'loves' it all!

Oh yes! There is one more thing about the SN thing. When I say to people I don't use it because I loath it, do you know what many of them say to me? 'Oh I hate it too, but you've got to do it these days haven't you?

Is that really so?

Section 8: IS IT VALUABLE?

One of the most important parts of finding your Authentic self is discovering what you value most in life. Knowing what is important to you will give you the indicators as to how to conduct yourself, what directions to choose and what decisions to make. If you don't know what your values are then you may be floundering around for a long time constantly trying out new things only to find them as unrewarding as the first thing that you started with.

You may, for example, choose a job that has some great things going for it but somehow you find it unfulfilling. You may find yourself in a relationship that just isn't working. You may spend evenings out with friends wondering why you are really very bored. Once you know what is important to you, you are then able to assess whether you are living in a way that is congruent with those values.

Let me explain a little more. If you value 'freedom' very highly but are working within a 9–5 job which is hot on deadlines and rules then you may find yourself feeling claustrophobic and not really knowing why. You may struggle to do your job well and may like certain parts of the job but fundamentally the '9–5' plus the 'deadlines' plus the 'rules' may just be too much for that internal sense of freedom that you need so much. We can all compromise to a certain extent but if there is more compromise than fitting in with our values than we will begin to suffer on every level.

Story-time!

The day I began school at 4 years of age I knew what I wanted to do. From very early on I was perceptive and wanted to help people to be the best they could be. I have a fond memory of being in the school playground where a friend and I had made up a game in which I had to rescue the fairy princess from the high castle. I remember pacing round the tarmac saying, '*I must have wisdom, I must have wisdom, I must have wisdom*' over and over again! I think that was the early sign of a value creeping in!

Later on in my school life I met the wonderful Mrs White who had a profound effect on me and there the influence began. I wanted to be a teacher. It seemed to be the best way to help people so imagine my surprise when, having qualified as a teacher, I went into my first job and hated it! Not that I admitted it to anyone mind you. I put on the smiley mask which said 'I love this job' and suffered several years of sheer hell which ended in a virtual nervous breakdown.

It wasn't until I discovered that one of my top values was 'freedom' that I realized that all of the constraints of the classroom were crippling me. I thought back to my own school days which I had also hated. Endless rules; ways to be, ways to think, what to wear, what to eat, when to start, when to finish, how to think…even the building itself contributed to fight against my awesome value of freedom. It also went against the value of wisdom because school is about knowledge not wisdom.

So why did I become a teacher? As an intelligent young girl who went to a Grammar School, teaching was the expected path. Mrs White (bless her) didn't realize that she was showing the way and my parents (bless them also!) thought it was the 'obvious' thing for me to do!

My worst enemy however, was myself! I knew that I was more perceptive than most, I knew that my attitudes and opinions were very different from most other people, I knew that I wasn't happy but I couldn't admit it. 'I must have wisdom' had translated itself to 'I must do things the way everyone else does them even though it doesn't suit me and is making me ill!

Luckily – I escaped! I'm still using all of the abilities and skills that attracted me to teaching but now I do it my Authentic way.

Your Turn:
What Is Important To Me?

Write down the answers to the following questions:

a) What 10 things do you absolutely love doing?
   Why? And what do they each give you?

b) What would you spend your time doing if money was no object?

   Why? And what does it give you?

c) What did you want to be when you were a child?

   Why? And what would it have/does it, give you?

d) What would your Ideal Day look like?

   Why? And what does it give you?

e) What is important to you in life?
   Why? And what does it give you?

f) How would you like to live your life?
   Why? And what does it give you?

g) How would you like to make money?
   Why? And what does/would it give you?

h)   What are your private daydreams?
     Why? And what do they give you?

i) What makes you happy?
     Why? And what does each give you?

Now if you have written answers to all of these questions you should see some values popping up. Words like fun, enjoyment, achievement, recognition and so on. If you don't, then return to the questions and answer them in the light of uncovering some of your essential values. *Don't* edit yourself and *do* let yourself play with the questions.

When you have a list of words, underline them and find them on the table opposite. Put a tick in the first column of the table below, next to each one. Obviously this is not a definitive list since we are all different so if you have some that aren't in my list, just add them on to the bottom in the spaces provided. Try to find 15 in total from your questions and you may even want to add a few that haven't been covered by the questions.

When you have 15 ask yourself 'If I had to do without 5 of these, which would I be willing to compromise on?' Tick the 10 that you want to keep in the next column.

When you have 10 ask yourself 'If I had to do without 5 of these, which would I be willing to compromise on?' Tick the 5 that you want to keep in the next column.

Why did you need to close them down until you only had five? These represent the 5 values that are most important to you. They are essential to your life and should only be ignored at your peril. Here's an example:-

Whenever my husband and I look for somewhere new to live (and we've lived in a lot of places!) we have a list of criteria. Each property we look at, we do so with a view to how many of the criteria it fulfils. Sometimes we have had to compromise. To get the location at the price, we might have had to compromise. To get a large kitchen/diner we might have had to compromise and so on. It's exactly the same with values. For example my personal first 2 values are freedom and security.

		Out of those		
VALUES	**TICK 15**	**TICK 10**	**TICK 5**	
Abundance				
Achievement				
Ambition				
Challenge				
Charity				
Dignity				
Empathy				
Enjoyment				
Enthusiasm				
Equality				
Excellence				
Faith				
Family				
Freedom				
Friendship				
Honesty				
Hope				
Humility				
Independence				
Inner Harmony				
Integrity				
Joy				
Justice				
Kindness				
Leadership				
Love				
Loyalty				
Obedience				
Passion				
Power				
Purpose				
Recognition				
Relationships				
Respect				
Safety				
Security				
Self-worth				
Service				
Significance				
Simplicity				
Trust				
Truth				
Understanding				
Wealth				
Wholeness				

THESE 5 ARE YOUR MOST IMPORTANT VALUES

I'm sure that you can see how those two may not be the best bedfellows! Security (particularly financial) often comes more easily at a price that would cost me my freedom, so for a large part of my life I have had to compromise the security in order to have the freedom. However I have learnt to balance it in such a way that it hasn't meant the death of me!

Have a look at your list and see where clashes may occur but don't get disheartened – this can all be sorted out!

Your Turn:
Knowing Me, Knowing You Aha!

How did you interpret the phrase 'who I am'?

Other than your name, what 3 things do you tell a stranger about yourself?

Why do you choose those things?

Do you undersell yourself?

Do you exaggerate or lie?

How do you feel telling people about yourself?

What would you like to be able to tell people?

What would you like people to remember about you?

Story-time!

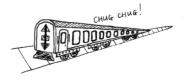

I was looking out of the window on a very long train journey when I became mesmerized by the movement of the power lines across the window. As the train moved, the line was high in the glass space at the point of the poles and slowly dropped down to the bottom of the window as it reached its low point. I found myself moving my head with the wire; up and down, up and down; up and down. It was rhythmic, soothing and calming. I was enjoying it. I had suspended my adult-self and was enjoying the motion in a childlike fashion.

Suddenly, I stepped out of myself and saw what other people must be seeing and in that moment I was concerned with other people's opinions. What must I look like? What must they think? Consequently I stopped a movement that was relaxing and true to me! Even despite the fact that I knew no one else on the train except my husband who is perfectly used to me 'doing my own thing'!

O.K. I admit that this may have been a different kind of behaviour for some people but so what? We worry far too much about being different. For me this small incident represented the degree to which we alter ourselves from our Authentic selves in order to accommodate other people and their opinions or to fit in with what we are told is socially acceptable. Hopefully next time I won't care so much and will enjoy waggling my head up and down with the power lines!

Section 9: BEING HONEST IN A DISHONEST WORLD

The big challenge with being your Authentic self is being honest in a dishonest world. This doesn't mean going around being tactless and aggressive but it does mean being willing to stand up and be counted. It does mean being willing to go against the grain/the flow/the tide. Whether it is in what you wear or what you feel or your opinions, you may want to have a different way of being than other people and sometimes this takes courage. However, the more honest you are the better things get for you. You stop saying 'yes' when you mean 'no'; you stop saying 'I can do that' and start saying 'what does that entail because my time is valuable to me.' You stop saying 'yes I'm fine' through gritted teeth and start saying 'actually that isn't good for me'; but more than all of this you start to relax your body, emotions, mind and spirit. The uphill battle begins to disappear. You start to develop clarity of vision. Your intuition strengthens. Your resolve becomes more powerful. You put up with less as you start to value who you are, what you are and what you can offer.

When your self-esteem begins to build even stronger you realize that there are more people out there to help you than you thought. As Paul McKenna says, you develop pronoia instead of paranoia. Pronoia means that just because you think that the world is out to help you doesn't mean it isn't! (Or words very much to that effect!)

Once you give up *forcing* the world to mould to you and begin to allow the world to change *with* you all manner of miracles begin to happen so let's begin that change NOW…

Your Turn:
Honesty Is The Best Policy

1. What one thing would you like to be deadly honest about?

2. It might be a confession that you need to get off your chest or at the opposite end of the scale you might like to wear the clothes that you choose out on a night with the girls rather than being bullied into what you feel you 'ought' to wear.

3. Decide what honesty means for you and what would be an appropriate honest action for you to take. Choose something that would make you feel good or fresh or washed or relieved or strong or happy or…

4. Write it down in your notebook. Write down the date and time that you will achieve it also. Decide now to do it to 100% of your ability and decide to have the best time doing it, whatever it is.

5. Write down what it will give afterwards. Write down how you will feel having done it. Write down why it would make a difference to you. Write down why this thing is IMPORTANT to you.

6. Decide on a small reward that you will give yourself for making this happen.

7. Good luck! I know that you will do it! And I applaud your courage!

Section 10: ARE YOU POSITIVE?

A quick word on positivity. Positive thinking has gone mad in recent years! I've heard people saying the most ludicrous things in the name of positivity!

Story-time!

I once attended a new age group where one of the attendees stated 'Oh if someone broke in and tried to rape me I would let him – it's only a body after all.'

I was horrified, then doubly horrified when I saw everyone in the room nodding their heads in agreement!

As far as I am concerned this is wrong on so many levels! I consider that all of my being is sacred; be it Spiritual, Mental, Emotional or Physical and I personally would not welcome mistreatment of any of them!

What about you?

Being positive does not mean going around ignoring all problems and challenges regardless. Putting on a 'brave face' or ignoring potential danger is simply being disrespectable to yourself. It's no good just burying your head in the sand in the hope that it will go away! The object of the Jagged Sharps and Fluffy Softs is not to see the positive in everything regardless – it is to transform the negativity into something positive.

Section 11: I SECOND THAT EMOTION!

I've lived a great deal of my early life being a Drama Queen! I make no bones about it! 'I'm a Scorpio!' I would cry, 'We Scorpio's feel things intensely and passionately!' Actually, little did I know that this was a serious misappropriation of Astrology! Astrology is simply a list of potentials not certainties! What you do with the information from your chart is up to you!

It's true that a Scorpio does feel things intensely and passionately but what I was doing wrong was not only was I identifying myself with my emotions one hundred percent but I was assuming that they were difficult traits to have! But we are not the sum total of our emotions. We <u>have</u> emotions; they are part of us and they give us an indication of what is going on in our lives but we don't have to identify with those that don't serve us.

Emotions ebb and flow. One minute we feel them very strongly and the next minute they have moved away. It's not possible to hold on to an emotion. The minute you do, your subconscious will challenge the strength of it. The next time that you are feeling low, take notice. When something distracts you the low feeling lifts and you find yourself forgetting that you were low! If you asked yourself, *do I really feel that low?* in that moment, the answer would be *no*. Have you ever been in a situation where maybe you've gone to work feeling pretty awful but you bump into a colleague who makes you laugh and before long you are laughing along? When the colleague goes away, so does your laughter. You then have to remind yourself that you were low and put on a low face! It's perfectly possible to 'do' depression simply by standing in a depressed way just like a new hairdo or dressing up can make us feel good.

Start to really look at your emotional states with absolute honesty. If you catch yourself 'doing' the negative states of worry, pain, anxiety, boredom, misery, jealousy and so on, ask yourself *"Who am I doing this for? Why do I need to show the world this emotion? What am I gaining?*

What do I need to change about my life to get the same thing but without making the emotion a dramatic moment?"

As I mentioned at the top of this section, in my younger days I was a big old Drama Queen! I 'did' the "my-life-is-so-much-worse-than-your-life" so well that I became a big old victim! However, it didn't serve me. Instead of making people feel sorry for me and give me the attention I required, it drove people away. I was considered 'high maintenance' and I caused trouble everywhere I went because I was constantly falling out with people trying to prove that 'my (painful) horse was blacker' than theirs! These days, I am much more honest about my emotions. I allow them to drift away in *their* own time rather than mine. In other words I don't hold them there. However, if a feeling rears up and just will not go away, then I know that I need to take notice.

Specific feelings and emotions regarding something that is happening in the present left unaddressed will cause all sorts of damage. Suppression is simply burying your head in the sand. Carrying around a smile which is fake will eventually lead to dis-ease of the physical level of self i.e. illness.

When something needs saying then say it. Tact and diplomacy is important for your own sense of wellbeing but don't sit on it; say it. This is where your own bottom lines come in. For a long time in my life I had no bottom lines. Whatever someone did or said was ok by me. Of course it really wasn't actually but I had a great grinning mask to compensate! The truth was that not only did I have no bottom lines but I also I didn't have enough self-esteem to say 'Sorry but that crosses my bottom line and I'm not comfortable with it.' If you make that kind of statement and the person still will not budge, then you have to ask yourself whether you want to have that person in your life. If someone crosses your bottom lines but you can overlook it and accept that is how they are going to be towards you, you will not feel any emotional damage. It's all to do with the acceptance. However, if you are going to feel really bad or angry every time they do the thing that upsets you, then you have to question their place in your life. Is it worth having them around to constantly churn up emotions that are unresourceful?

You may also still have negative emotions from past experiences. If you bring up a past memory and can still feel an emotion that you don't like they will need to be cleared or you are creating a Jagged Sharp which will block the energy from coming down from the spiritual into manifestation. There are many techniques for clearing these such as hypnotism, meditation, Neuro-Linguistic Programming (NLP), Time-Line Therapy, Emotional Freedom Technique, and Chakra realignment. The list is endless.

Your Turn: E-motion

Ask yourself (and write down the answers obviously!):-

What 'gets my goat'?

Who crosses my bottom lines?

In what way do I hold on to emotion?

Why do I keep bad feelings around when I should let it go?

What do I gain by keeping this feeling going?

How do I play 'victim'?

What am I going to do about it?

Your Turn: There Are Always Options
(or sometimes the best decision is the hardest but will bring the most reward)

1. Think of one area of your life that needs changing at the moment – somewhere that you are not being Authentic.

2. What are the signs that tell you that this is a problem?

3. What triggers off this problem?

4. Out of 10, what level is it at the moment?

5. What would you like it to be?

6. What would you like to happen? Be clear about it. What would you see, hear, think and feel if this thing changed?

7. What needs to happen (that you can control) for the situation to change?

8. How have you solved problems like this in the past?

9. What resources (skills/contacts/money/equipment) do you already have to solve the problem?

10. What <u>could</u> you do to solve it (not what will you do)? Write down 5 ideas and don't edit these ideas.

11. What would your best friend or partner suggest you do?

12. How would you feel if this was solved?

13. Which one of the options (at No. 10 above) will you use to solve it?

14. When will you do it (time, date)?

15. Well done you!

Section 12: ZONE OUT!

Here's how we are taught to think of courage:-

* ACQUIRE COURAGE ➡ do something great

do something amazing ⬅ get more courage

get even more courage ➡ ➡ ➡

⬅ ⬅ ⬅ do something spectacular

have unlimited courage etc, etc, etc,...

Do you know why you have waited for courage all of your life? Because it doesn't exist! There is nowhere you can go to buy a can of courage (or is there?! Does it still exist? If you are not of an age to know what I'm talking about, good for you!) The first part of the equation (*) is the problem. You cannot simply ACQUIRE COURAGE! We come into the world with a certain amount but according to our experiences as a child we will carry on building courage or stagnate or even lose our courage. But there is no value in being a victim. The past is the past and if you want to be who you were truly meant to be then the words of wisdom that you will need here are… in order to do something, you have to just do something!

The difference between those who do and those who don't is that those who do, do and those that don't, don't. It's that simple!

In order to be your real and unique self you may have to find that apparently elusive courage but there is an odd dichotomy related to being your Authentic self which will help you exponentially.

Many people live within their **Comfort Zone**. I'm sure you are familiar with this saying by now. It means that they live in such as way as to not rock the boat, not upset people and not cause themselves any grief.

When people talk of things as being way out of their comfort zones they are saying that it's something they feel they could never do. They remain in this state because it seems the easier option. They reason that if they don't aim high, they can't be frightened, disappointed or hurt.

| COMFORT ZONE | STRETCH ZONE | PANIC ZONE |

Now, if they do decide to do something different and go too far, that could be referred to as being in their **Panic Zone**. They have gone so far that they are scared out of their wits and may well be creating some unholy Jagged Sharps preventing them from ever wanting to do that thing again! For example, if you hate heights and decide to do a parachute jump to 'cure' yourself, you may well find that you have bitten off more than you can chew! Remember that we are all unique so this method would actually work for a percentage of people. However, it's not the favoured way for most people! Being in panic too often isn't healthy and might end up actually putting you off the very thing that you are trying to achieve.

Probably the best line of approach is to move into what could be referred to as the **Stretch Zone**. In other words it may be a bit scary at first but you feel that with a little support or practice you could do it. (Didn't your gym teacher always say that stretching was good for you?) You may feel a little apprehension but you have a real desire to do this thing which is your driving force. The thing is that when you try to do something different, it may feel a bit odd at first but here's the contradictory bit…the more you do it, the closer it becomes to fitting into your **Comfort Zone**! Before you know it, you are doing things that used to belong to your **Panic Zone** but which have now moved to **Stretch** and you feel totally capable of achieving it with a little help.

Moving into your Authentic self is just like this. You may truly want to do/be/have something but it feels too scary. It belongs anywhere but **Comfort**! But the more that you do the things that lie in **Stretch** then the further along the line they go! Before you know it you are tackling **Panic** (but feel like it's **Stretch** if you see what I mean)! The other weird thing is that behaving as your Authentic self, may require you to move into the slightly scary area of **Stretch** or even plunge head-first into **Panic** BUT – and here's the biggie – the very act of doing something that feels right for you will immediately alter the very nature of the experience that you have! By its very nature you will be feeling more comfortable with being YOU! Got your head round that one? Good! If not – reread this whole section until it is clear.

Your Turn: Comfortable Stretching!

What have you learnt about yourself that you know needs changing?

Which one area of your life could you start to move towards you real, Authentic self?

What one thing could you do that takes you into your stretch zone but would make you feel good if you did it?

When will you do this thing? (Write down a date and time)

How committed are you to keeping that appointment with yourself? (If it isn't 100% put this book down right now and give it to someone who will appreciate it!)

Which ZONE are you in right now?

Why?

Your Turn: Act Your Shoe Size!

This is a fun exercise which is about getting out of your Comfort Zone and getting into Stretch in a totally different kind of way! Don't be tempted to overlook it! In fact, I would suggest you buddy up for this one. Get a friend to do the exercise with you or at the very least make a decision on what each of you will do separately then keep each other to it! O.K.? Here we go…

Whatever your age, add together the two numbers. This will be your new age! So, if you are 25, your new age will be 7; 57 = 12; 60 = 6 and so on. Now decide on an activity that a young person of your new age would do. Did you notice that I said 'a person'? You are not deciding on something that you, at that age, would have done but anyone at that age might do. So for example:

If your new age is 10, you might decide to boogie on down with gay abandon in your bedroom singing into your hairbrush!

If your new age is 3, you might decide to eat some mashed potatoes with your fingers!

Get the picture? The world is your oyster and the only thing holding you back is your imagination! If you need to, ask other people (i.e. your buddy) to give you some ideas. It is entirely up to you what you do, but whatever you decide to do, enjoy it! Totally suspend your adult self and remember the pure joy of an activity which happens in the moment and with no fear of outside judgment. If you decide to judge yourself that is up to you but you will be breaking the rules of the game! Go enjoy!

Section 13: THE AQUARIAN AGE AND AUTHENTICITY

(Read this section even if you don't believe in Astrology! You may find it interesting plus it may take you out of your comfort zone, an essential for those seeking authenticity!)

What is known as 'The Ages' in astrology last approximately 2,000 years each. Each Age brings a new civilization, cultural change and often prophets or religious leaders. Whilst the astrological wheel of the year moves forwards – Aries, Taurus, Gemini and so on – the Ages appear to move backwards, hence we are exiting the Age of Pisces (Christianity with Jesus as the 'prophet' and the fish as the symbol) and entering into Aquarius. Due to the large number of years involved in the movement, no one can say for sure how long this changeover lasts or whether we have truly entered Aquarius yet but there are certainly some pretty compelling signs.

Traditionally, Aquarius is the ruler of electricity, computers, flight, democracy, freedom, humanitarianism, idealists, modernization, astrology, nervous disorders, rebels and rebellion. Other keywords and ideas associated with Aquarius are nonconformity, the unique, the bizarre, the unusual, individuality, philanthropy, truthfulness, perseverance, groups, humanity and irresolution. Can you see the connection between what is happening in the world today and the words to describe Aquarius?

There is plenty of evidence to say that we are entering, or indeed already in, the Age of Aquarius. The breaking down of fundamental structures such as economics, finance, politics and religion says it all. We are in a time of massive change which is effecting us all but people (and particularly those in power) fear change. Nevertheless, change must occur for growth and the struggle to keep equilibrium often means that there is a danger of 'dressing the same man in different clothes' as the saying goes rather than changing the man altogether.

This strategy is no longer good enough. Voids need to be created for new structures to be built. There is a need for thinking outside of the box, uniquely and with originality.

Although transformation must occur in the Aquarian Age, resolution may be difficult. The way in which change must happen may cause upset which is why personal strength is so important. Finding your own corner of possibilities in your own Authentic and unique way is essential but we must all also be aware of the greater whole. Because the bizarre thing about Aquarius (do you see what I did there?!) is that is has two apparently contradictory traits. One is the importance of the individual and the other is the importance of humanity. So the message here is that whilst we all need to rediscover our individuality, it's important to be aware of how that can fit into the larger mass of humanity. By all means meet up with like minds, shares ideas, celebrate life in whatever way you choose with others but do so in your own skin. The age of the follower, the cult, the matching uniform to tell which tribe you belong to, is over. Be a tribe of one! Stand up and be counted! I love the apparent contradictions of the Aquarian age; be individual within a group or network!

Ray Grasse, a leading astrologer explains that if you want to help yourself to move smoothly through the Aquarian Age, you should 'leave room for silence in your life; create a center in your life (preferably involving a connection to the **Absolute**); and resist the deadening of your world, so instead of filling up your life with manufactured goods or artificiality, bring living organic things into your life. Furthermore, you need to maintain a compassionate heart; be involved in a network or group; become more self-reliant; avoid being hypnotized by the "group trance"; and take control of your everyday attitudes (i.e., do not depend upon external events for your inner fulfillment).'

Astrology is a very useful tool for presenting us with a set of potentials or trends; what we then do with those potentials is up to our own free will. Fran Healy of Travis sang about being one in a million and we all are!

And there I rest my case m'lord!

Section 14: THE MASKS WE WEAR

Masks have always been an interesting concept to me.

Story-time!

I have done a great deal of work in the theatre and one of the strangest things I have come across in the world are the stories related to the power of the mask.

It is said that a mask has its own power. Once the wearer puts it on they become whatever is represented by the mask. It is said that the feeling can become so strong that it 'takes over' the personality of the wearer. There are stories of people donning the mask of an evil character and finding it very difficult to remove the mask once the play had finished.

I once played a comedy queen in a mask and when something happened on stage that shouldn't have, I found comedic words that covered the mistake, coming out of my mouth which definitely weren't in the script!

It could be said that we all wear some kind of a mask. Mine might be said to be daughter, wife, mother (I have no children but I do have a very needy cat!), teacher, mentor, coach, writer and so on... These kinds of masks are parts of ourselves and just describe the things we are in our lives. It could even be argued that they aren't masks at all but words that describe what we 'do' in life. These are not the masks that I want us to concern ourselves with today. The kind of masks that I want to talk about, are the ones that we take on against our will. Like the evil one in the story I'm talking about the masks that we get stuck with, that we find we can't take off when the 'play' has finished.

Here are some that you may recognize:-

The 'putting on a brave face' mask

The 'biting the tongue' mask

The 'being a good person' mask

The 'I love you' mask

The 'pleasing the parent' mask

The 'I'm a content, happy person' mask

The 'I like my job' mask

The 'martyr to the cause' mask

The 'pleasing the boss' mask

Do any of these resonate with you?

Write them down in your notebook.

Can you think of any more that are worn by people you know?

Write them down in your notebook.

Can you think of any more that you wear?

Write them down in your notebook.

Write down anything else at all that occurs to you about masks.

Now – I'm not saying that we don't need to wear masks some times. Occasionally donning a mask is essential and appropriate but when we do not remove them and get stuck behind them we are asking for trouble.

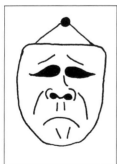

Whatever mask you find yourself wearing,

The REAL you should always shine through.

You should NEVER deviate from who you REALLY are.

Think about these statements:-

- The strongest person is the one who knows who they are, shows it and acts on it.
- You can only change yourself not other people.
- Changing your own state/mood will build Fluffy Soft's!
- If you have a problem, call it a 'challenge' and solve it.

Bearing them in mind, answer the following questions:-

1) Can you identify the wrong masks you are wearing?

2) In what way are you wearing the wrong mask?

3) What things do you need to change about yourself?

4) What situation do you need to improve/ change in order to stop wearing the wrong mask?

5) What needs improving/ changing that you find difficult to admit even to yourself?

Story-time!

When I was a child my mother told me a story. To this day I don't know whether it is true but it's a great urban myth if not!

There was an actress in the 50's who was determined that her face would never grow old. So she tended it with great care and when she acted she wouldn't show too much emotion for fear of causing crow's feet to appear. (I would say at this point that she couldn't have been much of an actress but witness the current botox era!)

Wherever she went she would appear with very little expression. Everyone remarked on her beauty although she seemed cold and unapproachable. She had developed the perfect mask.

At the relatively young age of 32 this actress died. Ironically she barely had time to develop any of those lines that she feared so greatly. Her mask didn't serve her at all. In fact, the strain of holding herself so rigid, may well have contributed to her demise.

What does this story say to you?

Your Turn: Do You Look Good Naked?!

These questions are to be answered in the light of self-discovery! Remember that the more honest you can be, the more that you will be in touch with all situations and aspects of your life! Try to be ruthlessly truthful even though you might have gremlins telling you not to write things down. You are only telling yourself the answers to these questions (although it might be interesting to reveal all to someone else!) I've used the word 'hate' in some cases which might be too strong for you. If it is just replace it with a word that suits you better.

What do you hate about yourself?
What do you really dislike doing?
What is the worst part of your life?
What would you do differently if you had the time again?
What drives you nuts?
Who would you cast out of your life if you could?
Who do you really dislike?
What do you tolerate?
Where do you hate going?
What else do you want to add to your list?
What's the solution?

Section 15: THE CONNECTION BETWEEN ANGER AND THE AUTHENTIC SELF

Anger is a great indicator that something is wrong with your unique and Authentic self.

Quick-fire anger happens when you break something or lash out at a fellow driver. Before you know it you are cursing and shouting and experiencing those distinctive physical sensations that represent fight or flight. All of that over a smashed cup or a car that isn't behaving in the way that you expected it to. It is not unhealthy to have a quick outburst but when that outburst changes your behaviour (i.e. you want to get revenge on that driver who cut you up or smash something else out of rage) then you are banking up anger and eventually it will come out in another way such as through illness or dis-ease. Anger sends the blood flowing through the body in negative ways and can actually reduce the I.Q. by 20 points! Not a great way to live is it?!

To deal with this sort of anger, ask yourself whether this incident is really important enough to be so dramatic? On a scale from 1–10 (with 1 being unimportant and 10 being death!) what does this aggravation really rate? Is it really so important as to give you palpitations? Will you remember it in 5 years time? Or even tomorrow? Does it really figure large in your life or are you just letting it take control of you?

If you continually get angry for no apparent reason and particularly when it's anger at petty things, it is worth looking at what it is that is really upsetting you. It is generally because something much more important is bothering you. You need to look deeper than just at the surface things because something is threatening your Authentic self. When you find yourself not being the 'real' you, it just becomes too much to bear and anger is the result.

If I personally get angry it is almost always a justice issue or when someone is being disrespectful. It is righteous anger.

Large scale righteous anger...

Many people experience large scale righteous anger. In other words the situation or issue touches on their own values or sense of what is decent, virtuous, moral, good, just, honourable or respectful. For example, a great many people care strongly about larger issues such as animal testing, loss of the rain forests, animal extinction and so on. In the main we generally find it acceptable to get angry about these sorts of things *providing* that our anger doesn't reach such obsessive proportions that the actions we take effects others in a negative way. For example; being so determined to release animals from labs back to the wild without considering the effect they may have to the indigenous wildlife, could be considered reckless. I don't think that any intelligent person would disagree with that.

The difficulty here is that we must remember that whatever someone believes it is *still* their personal opinion and that everyone is entitled to their own opinion. No matter how hard that is for us to accept, we must be respectful of a person's right to choose what they believe. We can choose to counteract it or attempt to educate them but our actions, however well-intentioned, should also be well-considered.

Smaller scale righteous anger...

This is where I feel that we have been wronged by *someone*. The same words apply here as they did to the larger scale righteous anger – decent, virtuous, moral, good, just, honourable, and respectful – but it becomes connected to our more personal values. If truth is high on my values (as indeed it is) then I would not take kindly to someone lying to me. I would get angry and would deal with the situation accordingly. It's also worth mentioning here that even though I regard myself as a 'spiritual' person that doesn't mean that I'm not going to show anger (and believe me I can be fierce!) My spiritual awareness is tightly wrapped up with my Authentic self and anger will out particularly if I am holding righteous anger. Maybe not straight away but if I have said something 3 times and I'm still not being heard then I will blow! So, those of you who know me – look back at those times when you've seen me angry and look at what the issues have been about…

Your Turn:
Angry? I Could Spit Feathers!

One way to find out what is happening (if you don't already know what is causing it) is by making a list. Start with the words 'I get angry at or when…' Writing down what frustrates and angers you can help you to clarify what is going on. If you start by writing down the minor irritations and keep going, before long the 'real' stuff will start to come through. You may be surprised at what you find that was hidden deep within your unconscious. It may require you to be brave because you may find some things need changing which at first frighten you. Pink Floyd sang about hanging on in quiet desperation but wouldn't you rather be free than trapped in a prison of your own discontent?

After writing your list, the next step is not to dwell on those things (that will only cause more anger!) but to begin to make steps to change those things in your life. You may have some things on your list such as 'other drivers being stupid on the roads.' It's important to realise that there some are things which are out of your control such as other people's behaviour. Identify these things first. You may not be able to change other people but the one thing that you can change in these cases is – your attitude. With the 'small' (but none-the-less irritating!) things ask yourself the questions mentioned earlier in this section. Get the situation in perspective. Letting go of minor irritations can be very easy once you get the hang of it. It is a learnt art but you do have to practice – just like anything else! Then focus on the really important things that are about your 'real', Authentic self, the self that wants to be let out and will show you how to go about it, if you just listen to your anger.

Section 16: YOU DON'T NEED TO BE A HEADLESS CHICKEN
(like Treacle the Cat!)

Authenticity isn't always about fast movement.

The word 'achieving' has come to mean; running around like a headless chicken, go-getting, fast-moving, forward motivation, speed, frenzy, goal-setting, constant activity. However, it's sometimes important to *achieve* stillness, peace, quiet, contemplation, tranquility, calm, pause, space, clarity, inactivity.

How much of each (activity and stillness) do you need? What serves you best and makes you a productive human being? I need a large percentage of quiet? Are you the same or different than me?

Life today is often about fast-paced movement. You are expected to do things fast. No one wants to wait (even though they may not even have something more important to move on to!) and patience and tolerance is disappearing. Along with the movement is the increase in sound; car horns, music, phones, car alarms, bleeping this and bleeping that. (No – I'm not swearing! I'm saying that a lot of things seem to bleep!) Some people thrive on this but some people don't.

If you are a person who can't take a lot of noise, pace, or conversation, or computer activity you are often considered an oddball. I have been 'old' all my life in that I've always needed a lot of sleep and like my own space and quiet. That doesn't mean that I can't party with the rest of them – I most certainly can! But I need to choose when I do those things. Going out for a raucous night of pint-downing and hilarity can seem like a blast if I'm up for it but if I'm not it's a trial and doesn't just put me in a bad mood, it actually makes my nerves jangle and I end up in bed for the next day feeling as though someone has pulled me through a mincer!

My experience has shown me that I am more sensitive to things than the average person whether it is noise or prescription tablets or certain brands of makeup. It's taken me a long time to realise this but now that I have, I structure my day to allow for it and ironically I can do more, if I do it in my own way.

The way that I discovered this was quite by chance. I was in the middle of Wales feeling very low indeed but I was there for a party. I was unbelievably tired but Daryl (my beloved hubby) and I had travelled so far for this party that I felt that I ought to go. It was the day of the party and we were ambling slowly around some bookshops when I came across a book by Dr Elaine N. Aron called 'The Highly Sensitive Person.' Reading the back cover, I discovered that her claim was that one in every 5 people is born with a heightened sensitivity which makes it hard for them to function effectively in a society dominated by excess and stress. All of my senses went on alert. I looked excitedly through the book especially at the list of 24 questions which could give you an indication of whether you fitted into her 20% bracket. I could tick 'yes' to about 20 of the questions!

Needless to say, I bought the book immediately, took it back to our hotel room and began to read. I read the entire book in double-quick time and Wow! It was absolutely me! What a revelation! All of my apparent 'strangeness' was in there! There for all to see, in black and white was all the reasons why I couldn't seem to function in the way that everyone else did! I was so excited that I overdid it and set my nerve endings jangling and very nearly passed out! (Yes – even excitement can set off my sensitivities!)

Now I'm not a person who generally favours labels. Labels can be an easy route to excuses and victim-city. For me they can be useful in giving you a starting point but from there I believe that we are still all individuals with individual traits. Labels do however, serve as a place to begin your journey. What you then do with that label is up to you. I decided that I would not label myself H.S.P. (her term for Highly Sensitive People) but instead I would live in the ways that would allow me to function at my optimum through the information on her pages. I'm pleased to say that my experiment has been a roaring success!

It has also made me question how we live our lives. If so many people (one fifth as Elaine Aron claims) appear to have the same sensitivities (and in my experience since reading the book the author is absolutely right) then it isn't about giving them yet another label; it's about accepting that WE ARE ALL DIFFERENT! It isn't just the colour of someone's skin, or their religion, or their creed, or their culture; it's every single cell of them! Isn't it at the heart of us all that we are supposed to live in an Authentic way? You cannot tell me that as large a number as 20% of the population should be considered different than the rest! What makes the 80% think that they are the 'normal' ones? But life has become about the 80% certainly in the Western world and for me it's certainly to society's detriment (not to mention mine).

I thank Elaine Aron for her research and insight and for having written this book and I can heartily recommend it to anyone who seems to be constantly in a state of anxiety and sensitivity. It might help you (though obviously it's no guarantee) but it also represents for me how far we've come from accepting people's inherent differences. We do not all fit some personality mould any more than we are all happy to drink fizzy pop!

So, taking you back to my original point of activity -v- stillness… it is vitally important for *everyone* to decide on their own percentage of fast-paced running around compared to their calm and quiet. What percentage balance do you need? How often do you need to just stop and regroup? How often would you say 'no' to that evening out, dinner, party, 'obligation' if your stillness is just as important as activity?

Personally I think Treacle the Cat has it sussed! What does he do after all of that manic running around? He sleeps. We've so much in common you and I Treacle!

Your Turn: Relaxez Vous!

Try this simple exercise for just a few minutes every day and see what a difference it makes to your life in a very short space of time.

1:

Sit somewhere you won't be disturbed for a few minutes (and that might have to be the loo if you are at work!)

Relax your body as much as you can

Take a deep breath in and let it out slowly and easily

Ignore all sounds around you

Take your focus from outside of yourself and put it inside of you

Gently be aware of your breathing in and out

Let your thoughts come and go. Try not to hold on to any thoughts

Do nothing more than that for a few minutes

2:

If you wish to move the exercise on a little then spend a few moments doing the above then

Take a few deep breaths in and out as follows:-

Place you hands on your waistline

As you breathe in to the count of 4 expand your belly to fill with your breath

Then, as you breathe out to the count of 8 contracting your belly to empty your breath

(Please note that these are only guidelines for you to count. Providing that you breathe out for longer than you are breathing in then you are doing fine. Don't get hung up on 'right' and 'wrong'!)

If you get dizzy at all, just stop. You will be able to do more as you become experienced at deep breathing.

Section 17: LACK-A-DAY!

When we are not being true to ourselves, things begin to go seriously awry. We each have our own version of things that make us groan. That thing which makes you feel that the plug has been pulled on your energy or that you are shrinking. Learn to recognise those things and to love them. They are telling you that something isn't right. I'm not talking about the groans that we all feel when we have to fill in yet another form; I'm referring to that deep one that comes from despair.

I put these into 5 categories which you can apply to whatever part of your life is affected whether it is work, relationships, playtime or all of the above!

Your Turn: The 5 Fundamental Lacks and their Solutions

1) The inability to remain true to yourself

Potentially leading to:- lower energy levels, excess stress, the inability to relax, wearing a constant 'mask', feelings of not 'fitting in', not living at an optimum pace and style, insufficient self-esteem

Solution:- practice releasing the 'real' you every day. Do or say just one thing that you wouldn't normally. Take a small risk and note the consequences. You will find the more you practice this, the better the reactions and you will gain more respect from being real.

2) Unclear and ineffective communication

Potentially leading to:- unresolved anger, the 'no-point-in-complaining' syndrome, unresolved personality problems, feelings of not being heard

Solution:- make a list of the things that you are putting up with. Remember that this is your opinion and you are entitled to it. Then set about solving one problem each day. Speak to someone who can make the changes that you need and by doing this on a regular basis you will feel more empowered. Be brave enough to say 'no' once in a while. It's surprising how quickly it becomes part of your Comfort Zone.

3) Lack of understanding of one's own actions and responses

Potentially leading to:- using alcohol as a relaxant, physical dis-ease, lack of confidence, 'burn-out', worka-holic syndrome

Solution:- actively make time for yourself. This is ALWAYS possible but you must make the choice to do it. Do something or go somewhere that makes you feel great. Recharge your batteries and then you will be much better equipped to face the challenges in your life and make the necessary changes.

4) The inability to recognise how other people operate

Potentially leading to:- irritability, impatience, intoler-ance, fractured lifeforce, 'hanging on in quiet desperation' syndrome

Solution:- go out of your way to understand someone else's situation. Ask questions. Knowing where someone else is 'coming from' will give you a better idea of why they may do what they do. Ironically, this allows you to avoid taking on everyone else's problems and focus on what your own needs are.

5) Insufficient courage to address difficult situations

Potentially leading to:- tension, 'putting-up-with' syndrome, demoralization, inability to 'switch off'

Solution:- each day, make a list of the things that you have to do. Grade them A) Most important and will move you on significantly, B) Need to do it but can be saved for another day, C) Not really of major importance.
The A)'s may well be the things that you procrastinate over the most. Do them immediately then enjoy the rest of your day!

Section 18: TRANSFORM THOSE JAGGED SHARPS!

(If you don't know what a Jagged Sharp is –
STOP SKIPPING THROUGH THIS BOOK!
Go back to Section 4)

I mentioned earlier that A Jagged Sharp could be called a Limiting Belief; in other words it is a thought which is preventing you from doing something that you want to do or moving forward. Remember that they are like big bits of sharp, dark glass preventing the thought from moving through the river. They plunge you into a darkness which is hard to navigate. I should think by know whilst working through this book, you have come across a few of your own.

Here are a few Limiting Beliefs from my past that have proved to be untrue:-

An apple a day keeps the doctor away
The moon is made of cheese
Carrots will make you see in the dark
My dad knows the answer to every question
Doctors never lie

Now, most of these haven't caused a great deal of a problem; it's disappointing that my dad doesn't know everything but there you go, that's life!

However, the following list has caused no end of problems. These are casual comments that people have made (granted, some of them repeatedly) that have 'stuck' in my subconscious causing Jagged Sharps:-

'...the way you live your life...'
'Why do you have to be different?'
'That's just not normal.'
'...Scorpio's are so volatile...'
'Who do you think you are?'
'How dare you!'
'You're stupid!'

Let me explain:-

'...the way you live your life...'

A comment made because I was a 'creative' person who didn't want to have a 9–5 job and enjoyed following my passions. This came from someone who spent 20 years in a suit travelling miles every day to a job he hated. His perception of life was that everyone 'should' have a long-term stable job which you didn't necessarily like. Although I didn't agree, for a long time I felt as though I was the 'abnormal' one.

'Why do you have to be different?'

Because I didn't want to paint my walls magnolia as this person did but instead chose a vibrant red.

'...Scorpio's are so volatile...'

This gem came from an Astrology teacher who should have known better. There is a big difference between volatile (with all of its dark, dangerous and negative connotations) and deeply passionate and intense. She was an emotionally cool Aquarian who would see almost any emotional expression as a bit hairy!

'Who do you think you are?'

From a person displaying 'tall poppy syndrome'. If you've never heard this expression, it is the desire to cut down a poppy which grows higher than the others. In other words if you are doing well, you should be stopped in your tracks; a very popular syndrome with the British media.

'How dare you!'

This from a person who loved to control and thought it outrageous that I should even suggest paying for her lunch.

'You're stupid!'

This was from a 'friend' who apparently knew way more than I did about world affairs even though all I was trying to do was have a conversation with her and she had no facts or opinions to draw upon! Confused? So was I!

Now – I don't tell you all of these things to be a victim (although I was for a long while in my earlier life). I tell you them to show you how the most crass, insensitive, inane and obviously subjective things that people can say will still cause Jagged Sharps. Even though we intellectually know that their opinion doesn't really matter in the grand scheme of things or is ill-conceived, ill-informed or coming from their own personal fears about the world, they can still cause us emotional pain. They can still sit in that old subconscious for years causing trouble.

So what do we do about them? Well there are many ways to deal with these apparently unmovable thoughts. As mentioned before, they are many and various. I have tried many techniques myself and indeed, use many of them on both myself and clients. However, despite what anyone says, in my experience there is nothing in the world that works EVERY TIME for EVERYONE. You have to find a technique that you find appropriate, suitable and that you already have a degree of faith in. If you do not believe then IT WILL FAIL. I know that this will be a contentious issue for some people reading this book but I have witnessed this time and time again. The subconscious is all-powerful and if you have no wish for something to 'work' then IT SIMPLY WON'T!

Also if the reason for living with a Limiting Belief has a strong enough payoff, for example, it gives you attention, it makes you feel significant or special, it enables you to remain a drama-queen or a victim, you will not <u>allow</u> the change to occur! So decide from NOW that change is good. Getting rid of those fears and phobias and negative Jagged Sharps in your subconscious is going to make you feel great.

You won't need to be a drama queen or a victim because you will see the value of being your Authentic self – and loving it!

It's also worth mentioning that there isn't always a need for a 'technique'. Some Jagged Sharps will go of their own accord once you have realized that they exist. Taking action is often all that is required to dispel the Limiting Belief. It may mean a short trip into your Stretch Zone but remember that the more that you take that trip the quicker it becomes your Comfort Zone!

Story-time!

I had a boyfriend when I was 19 years old (a long time ago) who had all sorts of fears and phobias from balloons, to dentists, to carrier bags left on pavements, to people with pink eyelashes (OK so I made that one up!) Most of them actually weren't that deep-seated which is to say that he could quite easily have overcome them if he chose to. Believe me; I tested them out on a lot of occasions! For example he suddenly wasn't scared of balloons if someone important was in the room that he wanted to impress!

These apparent Jagged Sharps played a role. They made him feel special, unique and different and he obviously felt that he couldn't rely on his personality alone to do that. So everywhere we (me, him and our friends) went we all had to lend our attention to Himself constantly so that he didn't encounter any of these things and then we had to deal with the fallout if he did. At the time we put up with it all because fundamentally he was a good, honourable, generous guy and we loved him regardless. It was also easy to put it down to the folly of youth. By the time I moved on I had suffered some ignominious times but I accepted that as being part of the life spent with Himself!

Years later, I ran across him again (not literally!). By now we were both a good deal older and he was married, with a mortgage and all of the accoutrements of adulthood. There was just one thing that hadn't remotely changed about this guy. He still had all of the old fears and 'phobias' from balloons to dentists to carrier bags and people with pink eyelashes (OK – I still made that one up!) Not only had he not attempted in adulthood to combat any of them but even though some of them weren't even real at the start, they were probably now all *very* real from the constant reinforcement that he gave them!

Your Turn: A Fluffy Soft Is Born!

By all means choose one of the methods that I mentioned previously to combat your Jagged Sharps but alongside that I have something for you to do!

Write down a Jagged Sharp that is <u>apparently</u> 'locked' in your subconscious. Maybe choose a thing that is based on something that someone has told you or something that you have done in the past that is preventing you from moving forward now. (Don't choose a phobia however).

Now write down what it would take to get rid of it. What would have to happen for you to accept that it is now a distant memory? For example if you've chosen an opinion that needs to be counteracted, write down whose opinion do you need to get now to change the one that is apparently 'locked' in your subconscious? Whose opinion would be important enough to you or that you could trust? Is your Jagged Sharp something that actually you could talk yourself out of if you were honest i.e. maybe it isn't really that deep-rooted? Do you need to take some sort of action to get rid of this Jagged Sharp? How much would you have to do to change that JS?

Write down how great it would feel to be rid of this Jagged Sharp. What would you see, hear, speak, feel or experience if you could be rid of it? What would it mean to you? How would you benefit? Who else would it affect? How would this be good for them?

Break down your JS's by doing something to totally disprove them and eradicate them from existence! The new action or experience will create Fluffy Soft's galore and all you need to do is repeat those to bed them in!

Now – BABY! GO DO YOUR THANG!

Your Turn:
You're A Hard Habit To Break!

JS's also show up as habits. You've done it so often that way that you believe that you can't change this thing. Your Authentic self cannot grow if bad habits are stopping it. Change routines, apply the exercise above and create wonderful Fluffy Softs!

Your Turn: I Dare You!

Choose one dare for yourself (or maybe ask a good friend to choose one for you; make it someone you trust and who knows you well.)

Choose a dare that you can feasibly organize in a week.

Choose a dare that is challenging, but would be fun or rewarding to achieve.

Choose something that you feel in your heart is Authentically you, but which would pop you a little into your Stretch Zone to achieve. (I'm sure you can think of something but some favourites over the years have been:- going out in a wig, wearing an article of clothing that you would love to but never have, singing at karaoke, paint-balling or go-carting)

Decide and record in your notebook; when, where, how and with whom you will achieve this dare.

Go out and do it (maybe with that friend). As you do it, laugh about it! Enjoy the boldness of yourself! Revel in it! Immerse yourself in the fun of it! Chuckle at your nerve!

Afterwards, record immediately how you felt having achieved it. Maybe even ask your friend what they perceived about you and record that also.

Then record how different it feels when you can laugh and have fun with the dare.

Now, what can you do **in the same manner** which has a little more importance in your life?

Mini Story-time!

A friend said to me 'I could never go out without makeup.'

I replied 'It would do you good to go out without makeup.'

She again said to me 'I could never go out without makeup.'

I pointedly repeated 'It would do you good to go out without makeup.'

She replied 'But I couldn't be seen without it.'

Section 19: THE MONEY TRAP

'**M**oney is the root of all evil.' Have you heard that one before? As a society we have been led to believe that money is a bad thing. We are led to believe that it will bring disaster, lose you friends, break up relationships and is generally a creation of the Devil. This, however, is a pretty warped view of the green stuff. **BREAKING NEWS!** Money cannot 'do' anything all on its own. In fact, money is nothing more than an energy we all have to use (at the moment) to get by in this world. It is a man-made creation which we can potentially all have access to. I'm not suggesting that there isn't a large percentage of greed or misuse, we all know that there is; but in itself money is not evil. Unfortunately, it is the belief that money is the devil's work that prevents many people from having any. Consider these statements and sayings:

> Money is the root of all evil
> It's them and us; the rich and the poor
> The rich/poor divide is getting bigger
> I'll never be rich
> Filthy lucre
> Filthy rich
> I can only do that if I win the lottery
> They can afford it
> It's easy for them, they are stinking rich
> The cost of living
> I'm poor
> I can't afford it
> I'm not worth it
> I would feel guilty having money
> We're not all born with a silver spoon in our mouths

Which of these statements do you use or think of on a fairly regular basis? If you are thinking ANY of them, at all, you are creating a Jagged Sharp.

If you have a deep-rooted Jagged Sharp concerning money then you will find it very difficult to attract what you need in life. Any negative attitude towards money is telling your subconscious that you don't want or need it. The truth is that you need as much as you need and the amount that you require will be determined by your values and what you choose to do in your life. *No one* has a right to tell you that you can't make your own decision on this one.

To be your Authentic self, it is important that you remove yourself from monetising everything. Obviously we all have bills to pay but start to take pleasure in paying them. Be grateful for what you are exchanging your cash for. Don't dwell on the cost or create negativity around giving away your money for goods or services. This small change (no pun intended!) in your attitude towards money will begin to make a difference in your life. Not only will you stop feel 'poor' all of the time but you will also find yourself attracting money when you need it. Any desperation for money can rub out the designs for your future that you are creating, (much more about that later) so don't allow desperation in. Instead do the opposite by showing gratitude.

Creating Fluffy Softs around ANYTHING has an extraordinary effect. It not only changes your own attitude towards that thing but it has a strong effect on the energy of attraction. The world begins to mould itself to the pattern of your thinking. Don't just believe me. Ask anyone who considers they have plenty of money. Ask them how they feel about it and what their thoughts are about cash. You will discover that they enjoy it and appreciate it and if they stop doing that, or start to worry about losing it then they *will* lose it. This is why so many people who have a great deal of money have at some point lost it all only to make it all again!

Many people fall short of doing the things that they want to in life and being their Authentic self because of money. They become petrified to move out of that 'secure' job or an out-of-its-sell-by-date relationship for fear of losing cash. But look around you. How many people do you know that seem to be able to do anything regardless of what they earn? Who do you know that goes ahead with a seemingly outrageous plan despite not having any ready cash? Those people are living proof that it is attitude (and creating Fluffy Softs) not the luck of the draw that determines income.

Section 20:
DEEP DOWN YOU ARE PROBABLY ALREADY
MORE AUTHENTIC THAN YOU THINK YOU ARE

The irony is that deep inside most of us already has all the structure that we need to be Authentic. The trouble is that it is just buried too deep or we have too many Jagged Sharps getting in the way.

'I just want to make my family proud' is one of the saddest statements I ever hear. This opinion may be contentious because it's ingrained that we please our families but what if your family has very different values to you? What if their way of life is anathema to you? What if you would rather die than go into the family business?

What if...
What if...
What if...

To be truly comfortable in your own skin you need do things for yourself not for anyone else's approval. This can be hard sometimes but some of the best decisions are the hardest. (Have you heard that one before?!) Knowing your own needs and acting on them may require some assertiveness on your part and sometimes it may be important to say 'You may not understand me but these are my needs.'

Your Turn: How Lovely Are You?

1. Write down 5 qualities that you would love to possess.

2. Now for each one write as many situations that you can think of where you have used these qualities.

3. Do 5 more qualities.

4. Now tell me you're not wonderful!

Section 21: BALANCE IS KEY

In Hindu philosophy there is a belief that there are three ways of being; three states of existence; attitudes, vibrations or energy. They are known as the three Guṇas. Literally translated it means 'string' or 'a single thread or strand of a cord or twine'. The Guṇas work together and we fluctuate from one state to another constantly. The idea should be for us to move from the lowest state up to the highest state. The idea is to balance the Guṇas and to see everything as one and therefore treat everybody and everything in the same way.

This philosophy can be very useful when looking at the Authentic self particularly when it comes to looking at whether you are using your energy to the best of your ability.

Sattva Guṇa Keywords:-
Starting. Being.

Preservation, goodness, fearless, pure, generous, self controlled, gentle, truthful, peaceful, calm, happy, contented.

Rajas Guṇa Keywords:-
Changing. Doing.

Creation, activity, restless, agitated, stressed, overexcited, angry, lustful, hatred, greed, deceit, fickle, distracted, acquisitive.

Tamas Guṇa Keywords:-
Finishing. Having.

Destruction, inertia, boredom, laziness, ignorance, delusional, obscure, dark.

Your Turn: How's Your Balance?

Look at the keywords for each Guṇa again and jot down in your notebook anything that immediately springs to mind as you read through them.

Now look at these further keywords for each Guṇa:-

Sattva = Starting. Being.

Rajas = Changing. Doing.

Tamas = Finishing. Having.

What are you best at; starting, changing or finishing?

What are you worst at; starting, changing or finishing?

The first keyword is linked to the second. For example: if you are good at **Starting** you will be good at **Being** and if you are bad at **Finishing** you will be bad at **Having**.

What implications does this have for your Authenticity?

Section 22: 5 TOP TIPS FOR BEING YOUR AUTHENTIC SELF

1. **LISTEN CLOSELY TO YOUR INTUITION.**

   It will tell you when things are not right for you. When we are working against our Authentic self, something – quite often in our bodies – will tell us that what we are doing is not right. There are fundamentally only two feelings – good and bad. If you are feeling good about an action then you are probably on the right track. If you are feeling bad i.e. a feeling of dread or nausea or overwhelm, this is the time to question what you are doing and more importantly why you are doing it. Be aware however, that fear of moving forwards can sometimes disguise itself as 'bad' feelings. Looking deep within will give you the answer. Ask yourself this question 'is it something that just isn't 'right' for me or is it that I am afraid to step forward into what I know will ultimately lead to good things?'

2. **BE AWARE OF THE 'SHOULD' WORD!**

   To be truly Authentic, you need to put away other people's opinions of who you are and what you 'should' do. Well-meaning advice can be the most difficult thing to ignore especially from friends! However, listen to what they have to offer then make your own judgement on the effect that it will have on you. If they truly have your best interest at heart they will respect the fact that you have chosen to do something different.

3. **MAKE MISTAKES AND LEARN TO LAUGH!**

   <u>Don't</u> be afraid to laugh! Being your Authentic self sometimes means going out on a limb. Dare to be different! Treat it as an adventure and laugh! Other people will start to admire you for the things that you do particularly when they see that you are more content within yourself

and if you make a mistake i.e. do something that you thought was you but wasn't – laugh about it! In the grand scheme of things it won't be important. Better to have tried than to get stuck within a prison of someone else's making.

4. **REMEMBER YOUR CHILD-SELF DREAMS.**

Are you living them or have you given up on them? Childhood dreams tell us a lot about what we want from our lives. Within those tender yet unrestricted thoughts lay the seeds of what we find most important in life. Look back to those 'When I'm grown, I'm going to be/do/have…' things and ask yourself whether they are still things that you would love to have achieved. If they are, then go get 'em! When is NOW a good time to be Authentic?

And finally…

5. **NEVER GIVE UP.**

There will be times when you wonder whether it's all worth it. Stop right there! Authenticity is your natural way of being. You have simply got bogged down with life as we perceive it today. Your real self will love you for letting it out and other people will marvel at how confident and relaxed you are now that you are on your chosen path.

News Story-time!

A race began in 1983 in Australia known as The Westfield Sydney to Melbourne Ultra Marathon. The object was to run for eighteen hours then to sleep for six. It was reckoned that it would last for about 7 days.

A 61 year old potato farmer called Cliff Young decided to enter. He was a sheep runner just outside of Melbourne. When he arrived, he was wearing what other people may call totally inappropriate clothing. He was wearing overalls and gumboots!

All the press assumed it was a joke and went to interview him. 'Are you really going to enter this race?' they asked him. '

'Yes' Cliff Young replied.

'So who's your backer?' they persisted.

'I don't have one' he said

'Oh so you can't run' they concluded

'Oh yes I can' replied Cliff by now a little annoyed 'I've run sheep for 2-3 days for years, we didn't have a four wheel drive then so I had to get them back home that way.' With that Cliff Young got his number and moved along to the start-line of the race.

The race began, but instead of running, Cliff shuffled along in his gumboots! After 18 hours everyone stopped, set up camp and went to sleep. Cliff, however, kept going. Every time the other runners slept Cliff moved a little further on!

As a result, Cliff Young didn't sleep for the entire 875 kilometres and he also came in 1st place trimming 2 days off the expected time! He didn't know that you were supposed to run 18 hours and sleep for 6! He just did it the way he knew how – his Authentic way. You see, when he ran his sheep, he did it on foot and if they were scared by a storm they didn't stop to sleep so Cliff didn't either! He just applied the same principle here and imagined himself running his sheep.

Since that time many people have used the 'Young shuffle' and won races!

A true story!

Your Turn: Why Change?

Why make all of this effort to be your Authentic and true self?

Ask yourself the following questions:-

What are the positives of staying the same
– short-term/long-term?

What are the negatives of staying the same
– short-term/long-term?

What are the positives of changing
– short-term/long-term?

What are the negatives of changing
– short-term/long-term?

What would be great about achieving this?
(Benefits)

What will happen if you don't?
(Pain)

Need I say more?

Section 23: OBSTACLES OF COURSE!

In the course of your change into your Authentic self, you will encounter some obstacles. One of these will be people who won't 'let' you change. You see, if you change it can upset other people's equilibrium because they will now need to make changes to themselves in order to accept the changes in you! Some of your family, friends and acquaintances will accept this whilst others won't. You may be surprised by the people who will not accept the path you have chosen for yourself. Even long-term friends whom you thought would be forever in your life may not take the journey with you. If this is the case there is no point in trying to barn-storm your way through them emotionally and causing arguments by trying to change them. They will either come with you or not. Rather if something (or someone) gets in your way, go round it (them). Letting go of everything (and anyone) that is no longer serving your new Authentic self may be a painful process but in the long run it is vital to your movement forwards and you will live to be thankful for it. However, whilst this process of letting go may be considered collateral damage or negative fallout, there is also some FABULOUS positive fallout!

When you release all of the situations, processes, emotions, thoughts, habits and people that gave you the feeling of pushing something very heavy up a very steep hill, the positive fallout is massive relief! Letting go of what is no longer serving you makes you feel free and invigorated! But no one tells you this!

Play-time!

Characters: **Shuri**
                      Duncan

The year is 2001

The curtain rises on the characters sitting in the kitchen of Duncan's flat

Shuri: Why do I carry on meeting up with Sharon when I've got nothing in common with her and she's still doing the same old things she was 10 years ago?

Duncan: Nostalgia?

Curtain falls

Your Turn: Stop Pushing Up That Hill!

Fear is not a good reason to keep people or things in your life that should have been released a long time ago. Begin with letting go of one small thing and you will be surprised by how you feel. Maybe not immediately but you *will* feel the benefit if you stick with it. Consider which of the following needs to be released in your life:-

Possessions…
Thoughts…
Ways of doing things…
Habits …
Emotions…
Work…
People…
Ways of making money…

Be honest with yourself.
   In the categories above, what do you need to get rid of?

Which possession/which thought...?
Write them down.
Now add the one you that hurts you to think of letting it go.
What do you intend to do about it?
When?
How?

Your Turn: Go Hawaiian!

Whatever you have in your life is there because you have attracted it. You have no one else to blame but yourself! If you have a person or situation that is causing you particular problems and you are finding it difficult to release the emotion try healing the situation and yourself with an ancient Hawaiian system known as Ho'oponopono (pronounced Ho'o-pono-pono). Do this every day until the situation changes – and it will. It is an extraordinarily effective exercise!

1. Recognize and accept that whatever is happening to you is by your attraction; it the outcome of bad memories buried in your mind. Think of your Higher Self and say:

    I LOVE YOU

2. Regret whatever has happened by you to cause those bad memories.

    Think of your Higher Self and say:

    I'M SORRY

3. Ask your Higher Self to release those memories and free you and say:

    PLEASE FORGIVE ME

4. Speaking to your Higher Self say:

    THANK YOU

(Note: You can replace 'Higher Self' with Divine, God, Universe and so on; whatever you wish according to your belief system.)

Section 24: IT'S ONLY FREEDOM DARLING NOT ANARCHY!

Being Authentic to one person means wearing a Marks & Sparks twinset and pearls.

To another, it means jumping up and down for joy, in public in the middle of the street.

To yet another it means 'tinging' a till in Tesco's.

To another it means making millions but living in a shoebox on the M1!

Authenticity doesn't come ready-packaged. It is whatever <u>you</u> want it to be.

We are still hopelessly living in our draconian past if we put barriers up against the way we choose to live. Suppressing expressive traits or mannerisms, being afraid to laugh out loud or cry when necessary, is vital to feeling free. This is not anarchy that I'm advocating. I'm suggesting that we stop living a lie; that we stop expecting others to live in the same way as we want to; that we stop preventing others from being free to be unique and Authentic. Is that so much to ask? I don't think so.

Society places so much on 'normality'. The 'normal' way to behave, to speak, to act, to react. There is a 'right' way to do just about everything. But who wrote these rules? Certainly there was a good deal of writing about etiquette and manners in the Victorian era but that was an awfully long time ago! Now – don't get me wrong here. I'm not suggesting we all immediately turn into loutish brats and spit in the streets and hurl our wee out of top story windows! What I am saying is that we have lost the ability to express ourselves in a true and honest way without fearing condemnation from some quarter for not being 'proper'! It is particularly difficult here in England. Our 'stiff upper lip' attitude has a lot to answer for!

The grave irony of all of this is the fact that the restriction that we are now placing on people in the so-called civilized world with all our rigid rules, ridiculous regulations, loopy legislation, pipe dream political correctness and so on is creating rebellion and anarchy. The restricting bands of ties-that-bind are making criminals of us all. We can't move in case we break some new law snuck in under the radar in the dead of night (sometimes quite literally).

One of my mother's favourite sayings was 'Rules are made to be broken' and boy did she have some insight there! Now – there are two ways to see this comment. Say it with the emphasis on 'broken' and this implies that we should all go out immediately and break the law; now say it with a comma after 'made' and this implies that whenever a rule is made there will be someone to break it. It's the second one that interests me. The irony of this world is that we are totally obsessed with creating rules to live by but when someone is told they can't do something, what is the first thing that goes through their mind? For most people it's generally some form of a question. 'Really?' or 'Why?' perhaps being the favourites. Either way, it is a question with a challenge associated with it. Agreed not everyone will think this way but for a lot of people they would need to have a VERY good reason why they shouldn't do something or their mind will begin to focus on how many ways they can break that rule. Try it for yourself the next time someone tries to tell you what to do. You may not be happy with what goes through your mind but you may be surprised.

The point I'm making here is that too many rules can create too many challenges and therefore have the opposite effect. I'm not a person who wants to break the law but I do need to know the reasoning and methodology behind a rule. To simply say 'Because Brussels say so' isn't a good enough reason for me to accept that some bananas are too bendy!

Returning to a simpler way of living involving what you want for your Authentic self and living by your own rules (whilst being aware of those in place) is so much more productive. There are enough rules in the world; don't place more on yourself. BE who you are. Live in the way you choose to. Express yourself in your way and let the next person deal with their own Authentic self.

Story-time!

My brother Graham and I were waiting for my father to arrive. It was taking some time.

After about 5 minutes I looked up to find that Graham and I were pacing the room in opposite directions! As I moved from the wall to the window then turned, he moved from the window to the wall then turned! We met in the middle totally unaware of each other's movements!

I knew that I was getting a little anxious waiting for dad but I didn't really know how my brother was feeling. You see Gweny (My name for him. Don't ask me why! Possibly started by my mother but lost in the mists of time!) is 8 years my senior and is severely autistic. He doesn't communicate in the same way as me at all. He can't really form coherent sentences and will repeat things over and over again until you say them back to him. It's hard to tell whether he is happy or unhappy unless he is in the absolute extreme of the emotion. He just does his thing whilst I do mine and those things can be so different that, I've never really honestly felt that I was able to truly connect to him. However, at this point in time our 'things' that we each just did, were exactly in tune!

The thing is, Gweny's pacing is considered a trait of his autism; so what about mine...? Well there are definite times that I pace; when I am trying out a new song (I'm also a singer), when I'm on the phone, when I'm timing a speech or a workshop and obviously, when I'm anxious. Actually I pace quite a lot!

My brother is always being his Authentic self because he knows no other way to be. So did I learn to pace from Graham since he's older than me? Or is it a natural and Authentic thing I do? Is it a thing that comes from being housed in the same womb? It also got me questioning whether some traits that we glibly attribute to autism or Asperger's are actually another A – Authenticity!

Maybe I'll never know whether it was nature, nurture or just 'me' being me and I don't think it's important to know. It was just great to feel that, for that moment, I was totally in tune with my beloved brother whilst we were both being our Authentic selves!

Section 25: INTUIT YOUR UNIQUE SELF

So how do you know if you are being Authentic or not?

Well, firstly, don't try to intellectualise at all. If you start to employ too much of the grey matter then you will find yourself running round in circles. Next time there is a decision to be made, employ your intuition. If you aren't familiar with your intuition here's a clue – it's got more to do with your feelings than your thoughts.

Remember the 4 levels?

Spiritual
Mental
Emotional
Physical

The Spiritual self will try to send messages down to the Mental and Emotional self to tell you what you need to action (Physical) to fulfil the deeper part of yourself which is connected to the whole of humanity. The Mental and Emotional levels often try to counteract those desires by putting obstacles in the way. The Mental self goes round and round in circles trying to analyse the possibilities and the Emotional self throws up fears which may be associated to things in the past or concerns for the future. You could say that the Spiritual and Emotional selves are more closely connected and the Mental and Physical selves are more closely connected which is why we must look to the emotions even though there can be fears attached.

Our thoughts – although useful because they will help us to work out HOW to do what we want to do – can get us stuck in too big a rut. Over-analysis will kill an idea stone dead. It's the emotions that are more likely to give you the feelings that will tell you if you are on track. Here's how it works:-

Q: How do I know if I am being Authentic?

A: How does it feel? Right or not? Good or not?

Q: What about my fears?

A: Does the desire still kick in? Do you still feel that you want to do it? Would you want to get through the fears if you could? Would you do that thing if there were no fears attached?

Q: I don't know whether I want to do this thing because my family has always done it or whether it's my Authentic self speaking?

A: If you desire it, it doesn't matter WHAT or WHERE it has come from. You may discover later that it is based on nurture rather than nature but at least you will know. Sometimes we have to do things in life that we discover later to be not quite right for us in order to discover that they weren't quite right! However, remember 'We don't make mistakes we just have learnings'!

Section 26: LEARN TO LOVE MR NOW!

'Today is the first day of the rest of your life.' Remember that one? (Maybe you aren't old enough to!) It was coined in the 60's (a lot of good things came out of the 60's it would seem!) Never a truer word was said. Whatever has happened in the past, you have the capacity to change it NOW.

Remarkable Story-time!

Man in coma. Man wakes from coma and, having lost his memory, doesn't know who he is or what job he did. Looks in the mirror and thinks he's not bad looking so decides on a job. His friends all think he is mad but he goes away and makes a success of it anyway. He becomes a model; in his 'previous life' he'd been a builder! True story!

O.K. so it's not advisable to put yourself in a coma to achieve it! But what would happen if you woke up tomorrow morning and didn't know who you were or what you do in life?

What new decisions would you make in our man's situation? What would be open to you?

Your Turn: Walk A Mile...

Walk a mile in our man's shoes. Lay back and relax and let your mind go slowly into daydream mode. Now imagine waking up to a brand new life.

What will you do today?
Who will you spend time with?
What will you spend your time doing?
How would you choose to make money?
What would make you feel relaxed?
What would make you feel happy?
What would bring about contentment?
What would make you feel fulfilled?
Who will you choose to be?

From your daydream write down the answers to the following questions:

(a): **What is your area of least happiness and where is most change is needed?**
(b): **What would you like to see happening generally in that area?**
(c): **What specific thing would you like to achieve in, say, a month?**
(d): **What is or isn't happening right now?**
(e): **What could you do?**
(f): **What will you do and when?**
(g): **What percentage are you committed are to doing this/ these things?**
(h): **If not 100%, what needs to change in order to make it 100%?**

Your Turn: You-logy...

HERE LIES

WHAT GREAT THING WOULD
YOU LIKE TO BE
REMEMBERED FOR

WHAT QUALITIES DO YOU
HAVE THAT YOU LOVE?

WHY WILL PEOPLE BE
GLAD THEY KNEW YOU?

WHAT WOULD YOU BE GLAD
YOU RISKED?

WHAT HAVE YOU
WAITED LONG ENOUGH FOR?

WHY WOULD YOU WAIT TO
BE PUSHING UP THE
DAISIES...?!

'The past is history, tomorrow is a mystery today is a gift; that's why it's called the present.'

When is NOW the best time to be Authentic?

Live in the NOW.

Be aware and stay present.

All of these sayings herald the wonderful power of *this very moment*! Although we have a past, we do not need to live there. Although we need to plan for the future, it is not useful to live there! I like to think of it in this way... if you are driving down a road and constantly look behind you, sooner or later (and probably very much sooner!) you will steer yourself straight into a big old accident! Wrong way to go about your driving! Look where you are going and stay present in your car. That way you can see the road ahead and can change your gear or your course if you need to. **Be** in that car! Relish every moment that you are in the car, even the difficult ones because it is teaching you more about who you are and what you want to have happen on your road. Every moment will give you a clue as to what you need to do to be more true to yourself. (End of metaphor!)

It is also an absolute truth that if things aren't going so great in this present moment, trying to find some gratitude works wonders. No matter how difficult it is, be aware of the good and great, things, people, situations, attitudes that you do have in your life. The effect that this has on your subconscious is that it will create Fluffy Softs on which you can bounce your plans for a better future.

Your Turn: Mirror, Mirror...

Read the following guided mediation then sit and let your mind wander through it.

Or get a friend to read it for you.

Or read it, in your own words and with your own embellishments, onto a C.D. so that you can play it to yourself.

> Relax
> Become aware of your breathing
> Take a few deep breaths
> Imagine that you are standing at the foot of a beautiful mountain

Before you, are steps that lead all of the way up the
mountain to very top

The steps are shallow and easy to walk

You feel excited at the prospect of walking to the top of the
mountain

You take the first step, then another and another

As you are walking up the steps you become aware that
this climb appears to be completely effortless

Occasionally, you stop and drink in the wondrous view
around you

The further up the mountain you go, the further that you
want to go

The top of the mountain is now in sight; just a few more
steps

You reach the top, you see something a few paces ahead
of you

As you move towards it, you see that it is a mirror

You approach the mirror and look into it

The mirror reflects the best that you can be

It reflects the utter magnificence that is you

It reflects your Higher Self

It reflects your absolutely Authentic self

What are you wearing?

What are you doing?

What do you notice about yourself?

What does your face tell you about yourself?

Who are you?

What do you love about your reflection?

What is special about your life?

Who do you truly want to be?

Thank your Higher Self for its presence in your life

Agree to take that Authentic self back down the mountain
with you

Walk back to the steps

Begin to climb back down to the bottom of the mountain

As you retrace your steps feel the presence of your
Authentic self
Look at the wonderful scenery around you
Breathe deeply
Be thankful for this moment
Return to the foot of the mountain, turn and see the
journey that you have taken
Enjoy this moment

Section 27: CHANGING YOUR MIND

Story-time!

A relative had a bad trait that wasn't serving her.

She said 'But it's just who I am, I can't change'

I asked 'Can't you?'

She said 'No, I can't?'

Is she right?

Have a big, gold star if you said 'No' and start at the beginning of the book again if you said 'Yes'!

Ironically when you are trying to be your true self you often have to get rid of a whole shedload of traits that you have picked up along the way that are no longer serving you. Like some old dinosaur in a festering, cobweb-ridden corporate structure, you say with horror 'Change – I can't change!' as if someone was suggesting that you tear your left eye from it's socket and eat it! Well (Bong! Bong! Big Ben strikes again!) change is imperative if you are to truly get to who you feel deep down inside that you are.

Let me take you back to The River of the Mind. Change is often a fearful thing to a great deal of people...remember how easy it is to stay in your Comfort Zone even though it's hurting you? I can't count the number of times that someone has told me that they have a fear or a phobia and I've said 'I'm an NLP practitioner. I could get rid of that for you. Would you like me to try?' What do you think their answer was? 'Yes please I would love that'? If you think that, you would be wrong. It is almost invariably either 'No thanks' or they pretend they haven't heard me! Why, I ask myself, would you want to live in pain when you could be 'cured'?

The answer lies in the fact that we are creatures of habit and being 'comfortably numb' (thanks Pink Floyd) is certainly the English (and a lot of other nations') way. However, there is very little growth, expansion, learning or progress in being that dinosaur. We have forgotten how to think outside of the box.

Opinion rules us and comes from all directions. From parents who say 'can't' more times than any other word; from 'well-meaning' friends who say 'is that really advisable?'; from financiers who tell us 'you shouldn't do that in the current financial climate'; from banks who like to say 'no' ('computer says 'no'!); from the media who say 'don't chance it'; from politicians who say 'that's illegal' and so the list goes on endlessly. And what do we do? We listen to them!

A Zen Message
(Just thrown in because I felt like it!)

So the Zen master steps up to the hot dog cart and says: "make me one with everything".

The joke could have ended there (you might have to read it again), but this vendor is no fool...

He fixes the hot dog and hands it to the Zen master, who pays with a £20 note. The vendor puts the note in the cash drawer and closes it.

"Where's my change?" asks the Zen master.

The hot dog vendor responds: "change must come from within".

Author unknown - but it is funny isn't it!

From now on you need to remind yourself that these are only opinions and quite often they are very wrong. (Obviously, a law is a law. I'm not advocating being illegal!) Ask yourself how is it that so many businesses still thrive in a terrible financial climate or that someone with severe facial disfigurement still finds a soul mate or a young girl treks across half the worlds continents and returns home completely unharmed? Opinions may well be the death of more people than any actions could!

In order to make the vital changes that you need to make you must learn to ignore both unsolicited opinion and the little devil in your head who is determined to join in with it!

Your Turn:
Get Thee Behind Me Satan!

'Before the book, there's the idea. Before the idea, the habits of the mind in which it gestates' Robert S. Reddick (Fantasy author)

Decide to do something new and Authentic RIGHT NOW!

In the words of Napoleon Hill 'Reach decisions promptly, change decisions slowly.'

Write it down with the time, date and place.

Then, between now and the time that you do your thing, every time your mind starts to doubt that you can do it (either from personal fear or from external opinion), simply say 'Stop. Thank you but I don't need that piece of information right now. ' Every time the unresourceful thought comes into your head, say those words until your Authentic action is done. It is a practiced art but this VERY simple process DOES work.

Now use it for other thoughts that are unresourceful. This is just one way to change your mind. There are many others.

Note: Obviously if you have decided to walk barefoot in a shrug around the Himalayas any idiot would tell you that you have lost your marbles! Listen to them! There are exceptions to the rule but I'm guessing that you are not that stupid! Whatever you decide to do still needs due diligence on your part but… well – enough said I think!

Section 28: THE LEVEL OF SPIRITUALITY

- Change can happen in an instant
- You are the tool to make this happen
- The technique is to get out of your own way
- Learn to let go
- Be firmly in the present

There is a vitality, a life force, an energy, a quickening, that is translated through you into action. And because there is only one of you in all time, this expression is unique and if you block it, it will never exist through any other medium and be lost. The world will not have it. It is not your business to determine how good it is, nor how valuable, nor how it compares to other expressions. It is your business to keep the channel open. You do not even have to believe in yourself or your work. You have to keep open and aware directly to the urges that activate you. Keep the channel open.

Martha Graham

Your Turn: Your spirit level!

PURPOSE –
What inspires you?

PATH –
What do you really want from your life at this time?

PASSION –
What are you really passionate about?

PEACE –
What gives you peace?

PERSISTENCE –
What obstacles stand in your way?

PRACTICE –
What actions are you willing to implement in order to create change?

Now...

1. List the people who are an inspiration in your life
2. List the character traits that makes them inspirational to you
3. What can you do to emulate these people?

"Do you have the patience to wait until your mud settles and the water is clear? Can you remain unmoving until the right action arises by itself?"

Lao Tzu Tao-de-Ching

Section 29: RUN AWAY!
FEAR FOR YOUR LIFE!

Here's a saying you may have come across – 'you get more of what you focus on.' Another is 'Energy flows where the attention goes.'

Story-time!

A guy I used to know berated his wife for not religiously watching the evening news on television as he did. He was very rude about it and made her out to be stupid because she didn't want to. He asked her how was she going to know what was going on in the world?

His entire knowledge appeared to come from television programmes and he believed everything he read in the papers. He always voted for one political party. When I asked him why, his answer was simply 'Because I always have – and I always will.'

He may well have been the least Authentic person I have ever met. Steeped in fears (at 45 he considered he was 'too old' to change) and unable to think for himself. His whole world was totally based on the television and the papers. As a consequence he ended up in a job which was far below his talent (he had worked previously in a fairly high paid job with computers), with no wife (she left him not long after the incident above), living in one room in his 3-bedroomed rented house (the room where the computer was), drinking alcohol every night, miserable, with virtually nothing and no one in his life.

What good was his dedication to the world news doing him?

We have approximately 60,000 thoughts per day and every single one of those thoughts emits a frequency and when we are thinking, we are also creating.

Think of it like this. When you want to buy an article of clothing, you begin by deciding what that garment is going to be. Let's imagine for the moment that it's a winter coat that you need. You may decide simply to go out and see what you can find but more often than not (even though we may be unaware of it) we have our preferences. So, on a subconscious level – or even on a conscious level – you imagine its size, colour, design, the fabric it will be made of and so on. This creates a very pale blueprint in the mind (and you could even say in the ether if you wish to see it that way). Now if you decide that you can't afford the coat after all, that blueprint that you created will be too faint to bother with and will be thrown into the 'bin' of the mind. However, if you decide to go ahead and do your shopping the blueprint will be refined and refined with every coat that you look at. In other words it's a bit like drawing a design of the coat in your mind with a soft pencil and drawing over and over again with your pencil until the image becomes stronger and stronger. Each mark you make is creating darker and darker lines until it moves from being in the realm of the mind to being in the manifested realm. In other words, it becomes real. The more we focus on the thing we want the stronger the 'blueprint' becomes until it comes into reality. It is made manifest.

This concept is quite easy to accept when we are considering buying a winter coat or when we think about something that is at the forefront of our conscious mind. However, this process is CONSTANTLY working whether you are aware of it or not.

So, what happens if you 'get more of what you are focussing on' but what you are focussing on is a whole stack of negative stuff? Exactly the same thing happens. Constant repetition of a thought will bring about a self-fulfilling prophesy. Consider some of these sayings 'That's just my luck' or 'I never win raffles' or 'I can't do it; it's hopeless.' Every one of these statements is building a stronger and stronger image in your mind of failure…

How many of these type things do you say to yourself on a regular basis?

Whatever you constantly say to yourself or to others is sending out those frequencies and YOU WILL attract exactly what you have made in the blueprint of your mind whether it is a picture of a winter coat or a negative word; it's all images to the mind and that's not all…

If every inch of your mind is focussing on all of the no's and can't's, what are we creating? Yes – 'Jagged Sharps!' If your mind is cluttered with fears and worries and stress, there simply isn't any room for any Fluffy Softs! One of the major problems in today's world is that we are fed an extremely unhealthy diet of fear. We cannot turn round for some newspaper, television, radio, internet, so-called social network and, unfortunately, other people filling our heads with all of the dreadful things that are going on in the world. I'm sick of it; aren't you? I've had enough of it; haven't you? I want to change that; don't you?

Think about this logically. If you get more of what you focus on where does that leave the word 'awareness' in our lives? We are constantly told that we should be 'more aware' but all of the things that we are supposed to focus on appear to be negative! It's a case of serious overuse of the word. We are told to be aware of bad health, be aware of potential accidents and hazards, be aware of the horrors of the world. If we get more of what we focus on then where does information such as 'smoking kills' and 'one in every eight women get breast cancer' leave us?

OUR THOUGHTS MANIFEST OUR REALITY

On the deepest levels and in the grandest ways, we are manifesting our reality every day. I cannot stress this enough. Looking for something WILL manifest it. It is a self-fulfilling prophesy.

2-Stories time!

One:

When I was at school at the age of about 11 and before I was aware of the power of our thoughts, I had a young friend who wanted to know what appendicitis was all about. Yes – strange I know, but it was her particular thing. She talked about it and thought about it all of the time.

I can still remember her screams of pain as the teacher helped her out of class to the ambulance.

Coincidence or a decision she made to attract what she wanted (for whatever reason)?

Two:

At the age of 19 (this time after I was aware of the power of the mind) I was having trouble moving my hands properly. I was eventually diagnosed by the hospital consultant with arthritis. I was also experiencing bad stomach cramps and was diagnosed by the hospital consultant with diverticulitis.

I went home on both occasions and decided not have either of those things.

They went away.

Coincidence – or a decision I made?

In order to take control of your own mind and therefore what you manifest, you MUST turn away from the flood of negativity. The biggest force of negativity in our world today is the media. Even though there is an argument for knowing what is going on in the world, too much negativity becomes a conditioned state. If, every day, we are bombarded with negative images and opinions, not to mention being told what we should think, then we have very little chance of being our Authentic self. Our belief systems are more likely to be put in place by someone else rather than ourselves.

Remember that the subconscious takes in EVERYTHING that you do, see, hear, experience and it cannot tell the difference between what is real and imagined; it will make those dark lines that manifest reality whether you are aware of it or not. This is happening, not just on a personal level, but on the level of community, society and world. Make a firm decision NOW to be more cautious about what you take in and therefore what you build in your mind.

Section 30: *FOCUS YOUR ATTENTION*

To experience the world in a better way and really be free from all of the ties that bind you will need to expand your thinking. As I have said all of the way through this book, things are changing. We are on the verge of new ways of thinking, new behaviours, new attitudes.

As a person who is reading this book I consider you to be special. You want change or you would not have read this far. Therefore I would love you to join me in being one of the **Architects** of that change. So…

Can you rise to the challenge?
Are you willing to take a small risk to achieve extraordinary results?

I would like you to *want* to change a fundamental way of thinking <u>TODAY</u>. (Read that again please.)

Are you intrigued?
Are you willing to trust me?

O.K. I'll take that as a 'yes'.

Today – I would like you to want to transform the phrase 'Seeing is believing' into 'Believing is seeing.'

What do I mean by this? Well, you may have come upon the concept before but now I would like you to seriously consider this as your new Consciousness Paradigm.

Our current belief system (for the majority of people) says that we need everything around us for us to exist as a human being. We have lived by that framework for so long that it is very difficult for people to contemplate that it doesn't work that way. But whether you are stuck in old thinking or not doesn't alter the fact that research is now showing that the world simply does not work that way. We were fed a belief that isn't true (in good faith) and it was simpler just to accept it. As a result, it is now so firmly fixed in our subconscious minds that it is very difficult for a lot of people to shake it off. Transforming a whole way of thinking can be a massive challenge and some people simply don't want to rise to it. They don't want to rock the boat because it will bring about drastic change and will topple the balance of power. A great many people are terrified of this happening; particularly those in power and those who wield the world's money stick.

However – you are not scared. You are extraordinary. I know this because you are reading this book. You desire change and if you've got this far through the book then you will have begun to make changes. So my challenge to you is this – Are you prepared to practise this Consciousness Paradigm not just to make your own life better but to impact the world?

> Consider this quote by Danah Zohar from
> *'The Quantum Self'*:-
>
> 'Old intellectual habits die hard. The Newtonian categories of space, time, matter and causality are so deeply ingrained in our whole perception of reality that they colour every aspect of the way we think about life, and we can't easily imagine a world which mocks their reality.'

At the start of this book I asked you to open your mind to new ways of thinking? Well in the words of Dr Who 'Come on Rory; it's not rocket science, it's only quantum physics!' The new paradigm is being proved over and over again but it's taking a long time for the old ways to die out. Remember when we all believed the world was flat? Look at how that turned out!

This relatively new quantum discovery is that, contrary to the belief that we need everything around us for us to exist; actually everything around us exists because of us. *It* requires *us* in order to exist not vice versa. So going back to your mind and what is chooses to create, can you see that this goes much, much deeper than just this season's fashion wear; it is the very basis of the life that you have now. You designed your current existence and you built it. So – do you like your creation?

It is also a fact of the 'new' discovery that nothing is separate from anything else. We are all linked in a far greater way than we ever imagined when someone created the '6 degrees of Kevin Bacon' game! In fact, if any two things have 'touched' (and this doesn't only mean physically) in any way they will still have an effect on each other even though they are thousands of miles apart. The very core of our being is subtlety influenced by everything that crosses its path. Therefore our central energy exists in all time and all space and can be shaped by our thoughts, feelings, physical and spiritual selves, it is much more malleable than scientists ever realised.

So what does this actually mean in reality? It means that we are not milling around in a mire of uncontrollable fatalistic mud. Rather we are dancing in a rhythm of our own making i.e. what we believe we can see, we will see.

Story-time!

I was having some trouble manifesting money. So I decided to use a metaphor which appealed to me being a water-loving soul. I imagined a beach and when the tide flowed in it brought with it money which landed on the beach. I scooped up the money and threw all but a small amount back so that when the tide ebbed it took the cash with it.

For me, this represented the money that came to me, the amount that I was able to spend back and the amount that I would keep for a rainy day (keeping with the water metaphor!)

About a month later, I found myself taking a romantic moonlit stroll along a beach with my husband in the Ukraine. Suddenly I looked down where coins were scattered all over the sand! 'Oh my God' I cried 'It's my metaphor!' The crazy thing was that all of the coins amounted to about 5p in English money but I had still manifested money!

There and then I threw back most of the coins keeping a few aside for a rainy day!

Be careful not just <u>what</u> you wish for, but <u>how</u> you wish for it!

Your Turn: It's all in your mind

Now look at it like this –

As you can see, from what is written above, your thoughts shape your world. When you want something it is like taking a soft pencil and drawing it (or writing it) on the moveable and malleable mists of your mind. Every time you think about it with pleasure you are taking the pencil and making the line stronger and thicker. But if you think about it with doubt you are taking an eraser and rubbing out the last line. In order for the thing to manifest it has to reach a certain strength and depth of line. It will never do this if you fret (rub out), worry (rub out), get desperate (rub out). It will only achieve strength if you believe in its potential existence gently but assertively. Act as if something is true even if you are challenged by the thought. You do not need to be focussing like mad every minute of the day. Ironically, doing that will create a suggestion to your subconscious that you are desperate and therefore don't actually believe in the possibility (rub out).

Gently create something that you really desire to have, be or happen, then wait. Some things can happen in an instant because you are not doing any rubbing out! Others are a bit like being on a diet. You feel good and positive (draw), then you doubt that you can lose the weight (rub out), then you have a few great days (draw) then you blowout on a heavy curry (rub out) and so on. The thing with this is that the more you rub out the longer the effect will be just like the not very successful diet. You may have to wait for 4 weeks until you see the result.

Remember also that all of this work is going on at a subconscious level so may be totally unaware of the number of ways (let alone times!) that you go to and fro with your pencil and rubber! Have patience. Which takes me back to our friend Ann almost at the start of this book. Have the Need/Desire, then let your imagination go to work on it, then take any appropriate action needed and this bit is key. It's absolutely no good waiting to win the lotto if you don't buy a ticket! Give yourself the best chance of manifesting your desires by taking action. You don't need to go frantic, or work your fingers to the bone, but you do need to help the energy to manifest from the Spiritual, through the Mental and Emotional and into the Physical.

So:-
What small thing would you like to bring about?

What small thing would you like to transform from an inspiration into manifestation?

Be sure that it is truly something that you want because you need to build Fluffy Softs not Jagged Sharps.

Go forth and be the architect of your chosen design and build, build, build!

Section 31: IT'S A WRAP!

Your Final Turn (for now): And where do you go from here?

1. Have you stopped falling down at least some holes in the sidewalk? (Autobiography Poem)
2. What has changed having read this book? (Sec 1)
3. What would you like to see happen from now on? (Sec 1)
4. What positive things did you get from reading it? (Sec 1)
5. What will you do now? (Sec 1)
6. Are you feeling more like a round peg in a round hole? (Sec 2)
7. How honest are you being with yourself and others? (Sec 3)
8. What Jagged Sharps have you now erased? (Sec 4)
9. What new Fluffy Softs do you still wish to create? (Sec 4)
10. In what way are you developing your Physical, Emotional, Mental and Spiritual levels? (Sec 5)
11. Do you have some basic tenets to live by? (Sec 6)
12. To what or whom have you begun to say 'no'? (Sec 7)
13. Which five values drive you most in life? (Sec 8)
14. How have you begun to stand up and be counted? (Sec 9)
15. Do you understand how positivity works? (Sec 10)
16. Are you aware of times when you let your emotions run away with you? (Sec 11)
17. In what ways do you now move into your stretch zone? (Sec 12)
18. Do you see how our world is on the brink of change? (Sec 13)
19. Do you always shine through the mask? (Sec 14)

20. Are you listening to your anger? (Sec 15)
21. How have you balanced your stillness with running around like Treacle the Cat? (Sec 16)
22. Do you allow yourself time to stop and relax? (Sec 16)
23. Have you paid attention to where you are lacking? (Sec 17)
24. Have you reviewed other people's opinions and whether you should listen to them? (Sec 18)
25. Have you broken at least one bad habit? (Sec 18)
26. How do you feel about money? (Sec 19)
27. Have you realized your good points and started using them? (Sec 20)
28. Have you started balancing your Being, Doing and Having? (Sec 21)
29. Are you listening to your intuition? (Sec 22)
30. Have you started to go round any obstacles in your way? (Sec 23)
31. Have you started to feel a greater sense of freedom? (Sec 24)
32. What area of your life still needs the most work? (Sec 25)
33. When are you fully in the present? (Sec 26)
34. Do you spend less time in a negative head-space? (Sec 27)
35. Do you know your greater purpose? (Sec 28)
36. Have you started focusing on the positive? (Sec 29)
37. Have you started to take on 'Believing Is Seeing? (Sec 30)
38. Do you want to learn more? (Sec 31)
39. Would you like to be an Architect of the future? (Sec 31)
40. Have you contacted me yet?! (Sec 31)

Now, having answered these questions, the main thing that I wish to stress is:-

DON'T LET ALL OF YOUR GOOD WORK DISAPPEAR!

CARRY ON THE WORK THAT YOU HAVE STARTED!

**REMEMBER THAT TODAY IS THE FIRST DAY
OF THE REST OF YOUR LIFE!**

Although you have come to the end of the book, this is just the start on so many different levels:-

If you would like more to read, there are more books.

If you would like to experience this work firsthand, there are workshops and courses.

If you want to work privately and in your own time on more in this vein, there are online courses.

If you want a foundation course that gives you a solid grounding in Authenticity and how to make inroads to your higher self and its purpose then there is a taster course.

If you want an in-depth long-term course that will make a REALLY SIGNIFICANT difference to your life, there is the **Harmonic Consciousness University**.

So…

If you would like to be an **Architect of Consciousness** alongside me, then I would *love* to hear from you. Change is needed in this world and I am always looking for dedicated and committed individuals and groups to continue the process. Don't worry if you are not sure how you fit into the process; if the things talked about in this book resonate with you and you feel that it fits in with your Authentic pathway then please contact me.

All that is left for me to say is…

CONGRATULATIONS!

I have so enjoyed writing this book for you and having your company whilst you've been reading it so congratulations for finishing it and for completing the questions!

I can't wait to hear from you and to work with you making not just a more Authentic you but a more Authentic world!

Until we meet again – much love to you

Shuri Morgan-Radford

FURTHER READING

Over the course of my life, I have a massive list of books that I have loved! Since I can't recommend every single one, here is a list which you may find interesting! Enjoy!

'The Highly Sensitive Person' by Elaine N. Aron

'Freedom Is' by Brandon Bays

'The Spontaneous Healing of Belief' by Gregg Braden

'The Power Book' by Dawn Breslin

'The Secret of Letting Go' by Guy Finley

'Feel the Fear and Do It Anyway' by Susan Jeffers

'Think and Grow Rich' by Napoleon Hill

'Loving What Is' by Byron Katie

'The Round Art (Astrology) by A.T. Mann

'NLP Workbook' by Joseph O'Connor

'The Compleat Astrologer' by Derek & Julia Parker

'Reiki For Life' by Penelope Quest

'The Field' by Lynne McTaggart

'The Intention Experiment' by Lynne McTaggart

'The Bond' by Lynne McTaggart

'Zero Limits by Dr. Joe Vitale and Dr Hew Len

'The Quantum Self by Danah Zohar